THE POLITICS
OF POLICY
MAKING IN
DEFENSE AND
FOREIGN AFFAIRS

Harper's American Political Behavior Series
Under the Editorship of DAVID J. DANELSKI

HARPER & ROW, PUBLISHERS
New York, Evanston, San Francisco, London

THE POLITICS OF POLICY MAKING IN DEFENSE AND FOREIGN AFFAIRS

ROGER HILSMAN

Columbia University

THE POLITICS OF POLICY MAKING IN DEFENSE AND FOREIGN AFFAIRS

Copyright © 1971 by Roger Hilsman

Standard Book Number: 06-042836-8

Library of Congress Catalog Card Number: 77-148450

To the students of Columbia University,

from whom I have learned much

CONTENTS

PREFACE

POLITICAL science textbooks and courses in the past have focused on the structure of government, on such matters as how the government, the Congress, and political parties are organized and on their relationship to one another. Recently, however, attention has turned to the outputs of government, to policy, and to the process by which policy is made. Who makes policy? Is there a power elite? How do policy makers work? What pressures are on them? Who has power and what kind of power over the different areas of policy? Does the President make policy? The Congress? Members of the Cabinet? Bureaucrats down the line? The press? Interest groups? The electorate? If each of these does indeed make a contribution to policy outputs, what is the process by which they interact?

This book focuses on this subject—the process of policy making—in the field of foreign and defense policy. It tries to place foreign policy and its making in the broader context of the workings of American politics and government.

Some of the chapters have been adapted from my earlier book, *To Move a Nation,* and I have also drawn on various articles I have written on the subject. Most of the chapters, however, are entirely new.

My thanks go to David J. Danelski, who read the entire manuscript, to Josephine Cuneo, who did the typing and various research chores, and to Hoyt R. Hilsman, who did the index.

The Institute of War and Peace Studies
School of International Affairs
Columbia University

This book was prepared under the sponsorship of
The Institute of War and Peace Studies
of Columbia University's School of International Affairs

In addition to *The Politics of Policy Making in Defense and Foreign Affairs,* the Institute of War and Peace Studies has sponsored the publication of works in international relations, international institutions, and American foreign and military policy. Among its studies of policy and the policy process are *The Common Defense* by Samuel P. Huntington; *Strategy, Politics and Defense Budgets* by Warner R. Schilling, Paul Y. Hammond, and Glenn H. Snyder; *Stockpiling Strategic Materials* by Glenn H. Snyder; *The Politics of Military Unification* by Demetrios Caraley; *NATO and the Range of American Choice* by William T. R. Fox and Annette Baker Fox; *To Move a Nation* by Roger Hilsman; *Asia and United States Policy* by Wayne A. Wilcox; *How Nations Behave* by Louis Henkin; and *The Politics of Weapons Innovation: The Thor-Jupiter Controversy* by Michael H. Armacost.

ONE
THE PROCESS OF POLICY MAKING

THE members of the Cabinet," Calvin Coolidge's Vice President, Charles G. Dawes, once said, "are a President's natural enemies."

President Truman, as he contemplated turning the Presidency over to Dwight D. Eisenhower following the election of 1952, used to say, "He'll sit here and he'll say, 'Do this! Do that!' And nothing will happen. Poor Ike—it won't be a bit like the Army."[1]

President Kennedy, on more than one occasion when friends made policy suggestions or offered criticisms, used to say, "Well, I agree with you, but I'm not sure the government will."

Once at a press conference, Kennedy surprised his aides by answering a question about allied trade with Cuba with a promise to put in effect certain measures that were still under discussion. "Well!" he said afterward with some exasperation, "Today I actually made a little policy!"

On still another occasion, President Kennedy had held many meetings of the National Security Council trying to get agreement on a policy for dealing with the Buddhist crisis in Vietnam. Finally, in one morning meeting

---

[1] Richard E. Neustadt, *Presidential Power*, 1960, p. 9.

1

several decisions were made that seemed to mark a watershed. After the meeting Secretary of Defense Robert S. McNamara, the Chairman of the Joint Chiefs of Staff, Maxwell D. Taylor, Presidential Assistants McGeorge Bundy and Michael V. Forrestal, and I (then serving as Assistant Secretary of State for Far Eastern Affairs), repaired to the Situation Room just off Bundy's office in the basement of the White House to draft a cable reflecting the decisions. We were finished by early afternoon, but by that time the President was involved with thirty or forty congressmen in a bill-signing ceremony, and only Bundy, Forrestal, and I waited until he was free to get his final okay. The three of us trooped into his oval office through the curved side door from the room his private secretary, Mrs. Lincoln, occupied and found the President rocking away in his chair before the fireplace, reading and signing the last of a pile of letters. He looked up and grinned. "And now," he said, "we have the inner club."

Later I asked Bundy if what the President had meant was that we now had in one room the people who were really familiar with the problem. "Yes," said Bundy, "but also something more. It's a private joke of his. He meant that, but also that now we had together the people who had known all along what we would do about the problem, and who had been pulling and hauling, debating and discussing for no other purpose than to keep the government together, to get all the others to come around."

What this series of anecdotes illustrates is the fact that in spite of the great power they wield, Presidents can very rarely command, even within what is supposedly their most nearly absolute domain, the Executive branch. As Richard E. Neustadt once said, "Underneath our images of Presidents-in-boots, astride decisions, are the half-observed realities of Presidents-in-sneakers, stirrups in hand, trying to induce particular department heads, or congressmen, or senators to climb aboard."[2]

[2] Richard E. Neustadt, "White House and Whitehall," The Public Interest 2 (Winter 1966).

"Washington," Secretary of State Dean Rusk once said when a colleague had been cruelly and unfairly attacked in the press, "is an *evil* town." It is an evil town, but not because the people who inhabit it are evil by nature, but because of the struggle that is inherent in this fact that policy is not made by the President simply giving a command. Washington is the capital of the nation and the nerve center of the nation's power. Where power is, there also are conflict and turmoil. Thus the reasons that Washington is the way it is lie deep in the heart of both the nature of the business of Washington and of the political and governmental process by which that business is carried out.

DECISIONS

The business of Washington is making decisions that move a nation, decisions about the direction American society should take and decisions about how and where and for what purposes the awesome power—economic, political, and military —of this nation shall be used. The decisions are about social security and medicare and labor laws and the rules for conducting business and manufacture. Or they are about moving a nation toward war or peace—a test ban treaty, intervening in Vietnam, the UN in the Congo, or Soviet nuclear missiles in Cuba. Where the power to move a nation is, there also are the great decisions.

What is decided is policy. It is policy about problems and issues that may make or break powerful interests in our society—organized labor or the medical profession or the massive interests represented by the "military-industrial complex" that President Eisenhower warned about in his farewell address. Or it is policy that will cost American lives in some foreign jungle and result either in our continued survival and success as a nation or, conceivably, in our downfall in a nuclear holocaust that takes much of the rest of the world with us. In the business of Washington, the stakes are high.

THE PROCESS OF POLICY MAKING

The nature and importance of the business done in Washington are obvious. The process by which that business is done is more obscure.

As Americans, with our flair for the mechanical and love of efficiency combined with a moralistic Puritan heritage, we would like to think not only that policy making is a conscious and deliberate act, one of analyzing problems and systematically examining grand alternatives in all their implications, but also that the alternative chosen is aimed at achieving overarching ends that serve a high moral purpose. Evidence that there is confusion about goals or evidence that the goals themselves may be competing or mutually incompatible is disquieting, and we hear repeated calls for a renewed national purpose, for a unifying ideology with an appeal abroad that will rival communism, or for a national strategy that will fill both functions and set the guidelines for all policy. As Americans we think it only reasonable that the procedures for making national decisions should be orderly with clear lines of responsibility and authority. We assume that what we call the "decisions" of government are in fact decisions—discrete acts with recognizable beginnings and sharp, decisive endings. We like to think of policy as rationalized, in the economist's sense of the word, with each step leading logically and economically to the next. We want to be able to find out who makes decisions, to feel that they are the proper, official, and authorized persons, and to know that the really big decisions will be made at the top, by the President and his principal advisers in the formal assemblage of the Cabinet or the National Security Council and with the Congress exercising its full and formal powers. We feel that the entire decision-making process ought to be a dignified, even majestic progression, with each of the participants having roles and powers so well and precisely defined that they can be held accountable for their actions by their superiors and eventually by the electorate.

The reality, of course, is quite different. Put dramatically it could be argued that few, if any, of the decisions of government are either decisive or final. Very often policy is the sum of a congeries of separate or only vaguely related actions. On other occasions it is an uneasy, even internally inconsistent, compromise among competing goals or an incompatible mixture of alternative means for achieving a single goal. There is no systematic and comprehensive study of all the implications of the grand alternatives, nor can there be. A government does not decide to inaugurate the nuclear age, but only to try to build an atomic bomb before its enemy does. It does not make a formal decision to become a welfare state, but only to take each of a series of steps—to experiment with an income tax at some safely innocuous level like 3 percent, to alleviate the hardship of men who have lost their jobs in a depression with a few weeks of unemployment compensation, or to lighten the old age of industrial workers with a tentative program of social security benefits. Rather than through grand decisions on grand alternatives, policy changes seem to come through a series of slight modifications of existing policy, with the new policy emerging slowly and haltingly by small and usually tentative steps, a process of trial and error in which policy zigs and zags, reverses itself, and then moved forward in a series of incremental steps.[3] Sometimes policies are formulated and duly ratified only to be skewed to an entirely different direction and purpose by those carrying them out—or they are never carried out at all. And sometimes issues are endlessly debated with nothing at all being resolved until both the problem and the debaters disappear under the relentless pyramiding of events.

THE POWER OF THE PRESIDENT

Presidents, as we said above, can very rarely command. Mainly they maneuver, persuade, and pressure, using all the levers,

[3] See Charles E. Lindblom, "The Science of 'Muddling Through,'" *Public Administration Review* 19 (1959), and his book, *The Policy-Making Process* (1968).

powers, and influences they can muster to get the people concerned to come around.

Often they succeed, but sometimes they do not. Then they must either pay the political costs of public disunity or make some concession to achieve the unity of compromise. In the Kennedy Administration, for example, the State Department was convinced that high-level visits to Vietnam were politically bad. They felt, in particular, that visits by so important an official as Secretary of Defense McNamara would get United States prestige hooked too tightly to the roller coaster of events in Vietnam in spite of the fact that we had only limited influence on those events. Visits by such a high-ranking official would also tend to make a bad situation look even worse by showing our concern too openly. And finally such visits would tend to make a Vietnamese struggle conducted with only our aid and advice look in the world's eyes like a purely American war.

President Kennedy was only too well aware of these probable consequences, but in the circumstances he indicated that he was prepared to pay the price, for the only way of keeping the high military officers in the Pentagon from an increasingly public display of discontent with the President's decision not to enlarge the war was to keep the Secretary of Defense fully content with the policy. The only way to do that, apparently, was to let him see for himself.

On some occasions the President clearly makes the decision, even if he cannot make it exactly as he might wish. On other occasions the decision is just as clearly made by Congress. But in action after action, responsibility for decision is as fluid and restless as quicksilver, and there seems to be neither a person nor an organization on whom it can be fixed. At times the point of decision seems to have escaped into the labyrinth of governmental machinery, beyond layers and layers of bureaucracy. Other times it seems never to have reached the government, but to have remained in either the wider domain of a public opinion created by the press or in the narrower domain dominated by the maneuverings of special interests.

TURMOIL

Just as our desire to know who makes a decision is frustrated, so is our hope that the process of policy making will be dignified. A decision, in fact, may be little more than a signal that starts a public brawl by people who want to reverse it. President Eisenhower's "New Look" decision to concentrate on air power at the expense of ground forces, for example, had no visible result for the first year except semi-public fights with the Joint Chiefs of Staff, an eruption of the so-called Colonels' revolt, and frequent leaks of top secret information. The whole strategy was completely reversed when the Kennedy Administration came into responsibility in 1961, and the reversal was fought by the same technique of leaks, but this time it was Air Force rather than Army partisans doing the leaking. At the very beginning of the Kennedy Administration, for example, Rusk wrote McNamara a memorandum seeking an interdepartmental discussion of the basic problem, and a distorted version of the memo was promptly given to Air Force sympathizers in the press in an obvious attempt at sabotage.

Leaks, of course, are the first and most blatant signs of battle, and they are endemic in the policy process. When it became clear, for example, that the report of the Gaither Committee, set up by Eisenhower in 1957 to study civil defense in terms of the whole of nuclear strategy, would be critical of the "New Look" and the entire Eisenhower defense policy, the crucial battle between the different factions within the Administration took place, not on the substance of the report, but on the issue of whether there would be two hundred top secret copies of the report or only two. Everyone knew without saying so that if the President did not accept the Gaither Committee's recommendations, it might be possible to keep the report from leaking to the press if there were only two copies, but never if there were two hundred. The committee won the battle, and two hundred top secret copies were distributed within the Executive branch. The President did not accept the recommendations, and, sure enough, within a few days Chalmers Roberts of the *Washington Post* was able to write a story, covering almost two newspaper pages, that contained an accurate and comprehensive version of both the top secret report and its recommendations.

Not surprisingly, it was these continual leaks that especially puzzled and angered Eisenhower. "For some two years and three months," he said in 1955, "I have been plagued by inexplicable undiscovered leaks in this Government." But so are all Presidents, before and after Eisenhower. Not only are there leaks of secret information, but leaks that distort secret information so as to present a special view that is often totally false. There flows out of Washington a continuous stream of rumor, tales of bickering, speculation, stories of selfish interest, charges, and countercharges. Abusive rivalries arise between the government agencies engaged in making policy, and even within a single agency different factions battle, each seeking allies in other agencies, among the members of Congress, from interest associations, and among the press. Officialdom, whether civil or military, is hardly neutral. It speaks, and inevitably it speaks as an advocate. The Army battles for ground forces, the Air Force for bombers, the "Europe faction" in the State Department for policy benefiting NATO, and the "Africa faction" for anticolonialist polices unsettling to our relations with Europe. All these many interests, organizations, and institutions—inside and outside the government—are joined in a struggle over the goals of governmental policy and over the means by which these goals shall be achieved. Instead of unity, there is conflict. Instead of a majestic progression, there are erratic zigs and zags. Instead of clarity and decisiveness, there are tangle and turmoil; instead of order, confusion.

Sources of the turmoil

Even though we deplore the disorder and confusion, the seeming disloyalty of leaks, the noise and untidiness, and all the rest, it would be good to look more deeply into the nature of the process before condemning it.

Partly, of course, the turbulence comes from the nature of

our Constitution itself. As Richard E. Neustadt has pointed out, the Constitutional Convention of 1787 did not really create a government of "separated powers" as we have been taught, but a government of separated institutions sharing powers.[4] The Executive, for example, is clearly part of the legislative process. Almost all major bills today are drafted and put forward by the Executive department concerned, and the President still has the veto. The courts, too, legislate—much to the annoyance of many congressmen, especially die-hard segregationists. The Congress is equally involved in administration, in both its investigative function and its appropriation of money and oversight of spending. To a department or agency head, the Congress, with its power to reward and punish, is as much a boss as is the President. Some agency heads can build enough power on the Hill to put themselves beyond the reach of even a President's jurisdiction, as J. Edgar Hoover succeeded in doing with his job as Director of the FBI. Different institutions' sharing powers and getting involved in one anothers' business provide the checks and balances sought by the founding fathers and many other benefits besides. But they also contribute to the phenomenon of turbulence.

The multiplicity of actors

Still another dimension of turmoil is the now familiar fact that many more people are involved in the process of government than merely those who hold duly constituted official positions. It is no accident that the press, for example, is so often called the "fourth branch of government." The press plays a role in the process of governance. It performs functions that are a necessary part of the process and performs them sometimes well and sometimes badly.

There are also lobbies, the spokesmen of special interests of every kind and description from oil producers and farmers to the Navy League and Women Strike for Peace. The lobby-

---

[4] Richard E. Neustadt, "White House and White Hall," p. 33.

ists' efforts on Capitol Hill are more familiar, but they work just as hard to influence the Executive, although in different ways. In any case they play a role in the process of governance and perform necessary functions, often for good but sometimes for evil.

There are others who play a role. The academic world, the world of research in the universities, has an influence and participates in the process, both formally and informally. In the Presidential campaigns of 1960, 1964, and 1968, no candidate could be without his own team of university advisers. Most of the more effective senators on Capitol Hill have academic friends, experts in the universities, whom they regularly consult. And there is a whole new set of institutions doing research of all kinds on contract with the government, organizations staffed with people who have governmental clearances for secret work, but who are neither in the armed services nor the civil service. These are quasi-governmental organizations such as the RAND Corporation in Santa Monica, California, the Institute of Defense Analyses, in Washington, D. C., and the Hudson Institute, just outside New York City. All these people and organizations influence policy. Although not accountable to the electorate, they have power and are as much a part of the governmental process as the traditional Legislative, Judicial, and Executive branches of government. In sum, there are many more people involved in making policy than those who hold official positions, and they have more subtle ways for shaping policy.

Policy convictions

All this is only the beginning. Among the principal findings of a British government committee appointed to study the powers of ministers was that most men find it easier to go against their own pecuniary interests than they do to go against a deep conviction on policy. As we have said, in the business of Washington, the stakes are high and the issues fundamental, both to our society and to the question of war and peace for the entire world. In such circumstances it is not surprising that passions run strong and full. It is not even surprising that men occasionally feel so deeply that they take matters into their own hands, leaking secret materials to the Congress or the press in an attempt to force the President to adopt what they are convinced is the only right path, the salvation of the nation. When in the late 1950s, for example, intelligence officials leaked secret information foreshadowing an upcoming "missile gap" to Democratic senators and sympathetic members of the press, it was not because they were disloyal, but because they were deeply convinced that the nation was in peril. They had tried and failed to convince the top levels of the Eisenhower Administration of the validity of their projections, and they felt completely justified in taking matters into their own hands by going over the President's head to Congress, the press, and the public. The same thing happened during the debate over the antiballistic missile in the Nixon Administration. Proponents of the ABM were so convinced that the nation's security depended on deploying an ABM that they leaked secret material that tended to support their case. Opponents, on the other hand, were so convinced that deploying the weapon would imperil security by starting another round in the arms race that they leaked secret material that tended to support their case. It was conviction on policy that drove the individuals to take the action they did in both cases. But this is nothing new. It was also conviction on policy that led Colonel "Billy" Mitchell to provoke a court martial in the 1920s so he could present the case for air power to the nation at large. And so it has been throughout history. The motive for such deeds—for mankind's greatest achievements, but also, unhappily, for mankind's greatest crimes—has rarely been to benefit the individual, but for the glory of something the individual thinks of as bigger than himself: for his God, his nation, or his ideology.

There is nothing in this to nullify the point that selfish interests are also involved in these decisions, and that the decisions affect such powerful interests as labor, the farmer, the medical profession, and the military-industrial complex. But society is made up of its different parts, and it is not merely a rationalization when farmers, for example, argue that a healthy nation depends on a healthy agriculture. There is nothing wrong when the people of a democracy express their interests, their values, hopes, and fears through "interest" organizations. How else, save through some such hierarchy of representative organizations, can the needs and desires of so many millions of people be aggregated?

Nor is there anything wrong in the fact that the bureaucracy itself is divided, that it represents special interests, and that its parts speak as advocates, fighting hard for their constituencies. The Department of Labor is inevitably and rightly more oriented toward workingmen than management, the Bureau of Mines more toward extractive industry than the industrial users of minerals, the Children's Bureau more toward restrictions on employers than permissiveness. Indeed, some segments of society that are poorly organized for exercising leverage on either public opinion or the Congress would have a much smaller voice if the bureaucracy of the federal government did not represent their interests. For a long time, for example, the only voice raised in an attempt to try to improve the lot of migrant labor before it began to organize was in the bureaucracy. The results were not spectacular, but what improvements did come were due to them. Many of the long-range, more general interests of society as a whole have no other spokesman at all. In any case, the fact that the different parts of bureaucracy speak with different voices also contributes to the turbulence of the Washington scene.

Inadequacy of knowledge

Still another dimension of the confusion and turbulence of the policy-making process is the complexity of the problems and the inadequacy of our knowledge of how and why things work in the social affairs of men, our limited capacity to foresee developments that bring problems or to predict the consequences of whatever action we do take. Partly this is because there are so many different people taking part in the process, with goals and tactics of their own. But it is more than this. Partly, for example, it is simply lack of knowledge of cause and effect in social affairs. More and better understanding will not always or necessarily lead us to sure solutions to knotty problems, but it sometimes does. If our understanding of the workings of a modern industrial economy had been better in the 1920s, the Great Depression could very probably have been avoided. If our knowledge had been only slightly greater than it was in the 1930s, the measures to meet the Depression would probably have been more effective and quicker acting. Another example is World War II. Winston Churchill called it the "unnecessary war." By this he meant that if we had better understood what Hitler and Nazism were really about and particularly their compelling dynamism leading toward war, it would have been politically possible to take the necessary preventive measures. However hard and costly they might have been, those measures would have been better than the horror of what actually did occur.

When knowledge is inadequate, when problems are complex, and especially when they are also new, presenting a challenge with which there has been no experience, there is in such circumstances room to spare for disagreement, conflict, and turmoil. It is not the only cause of disagreement, much less the central cause, but it is one of them. McGeorge Bundy once said that policy in Vietnam was "the most divisive issue in the Kennedy administration." He meant *inside* the Administration, and he was right. The cause of the dissension was precisely inadequate understanding and a failure of analysis. Modern guerrilla warfare, as espoused in the Communist world, is internal war, an ambiguous aggression that avoids direct and open attack violating international frontiers, but combines terror, subversion, and political action with hit-and-run guerrilla raids and ambush. It is new to the Western world and not yet fully understood. In the Kennedy Administration there were those who saw it as a modified form of traditional war, but war nevertheless to be fought primarily with traditional military measures. Others saw guerrilla warfare as essentially political in nature, aimed at winning the people while terrorizing the government, and they believed that in fighting against a guerrilla insurgency military measures should be subordinated to political action. There was simply not enough knowledge and experience with such matters to prove who was right, and the struggle within the Administration became increasingly bitter. When President Johnson made Vietnam an American war in 1965, the whole country eventually was polarized on the same issue.

POLICY MAKING IS POLITICS

These are some of the facets of policy making—separate institutions sharing powers; the press, experts, and others who influence policy without holding formal power; selfish and unselfish interest groups that exert a different kind of power; the difficulties and complexities of analysis, prediction, and judgment. These many facets help to explain the turmoil, and they flag a warning to those who would be cynical about Washington or unhappy about the hurly-burly of policy making that is disquieting or even repugnant to so many. But the many facets do not completely explain even the surface phenomena of Washington, nor is what explanation they do give completely satisfying. As Americans we aspire to a rationalized system of government and policy making. This implies that a nation can pursue a single set of clearly perceived and generally agreed-to goals, just as a business organization is supposed to pursue profits. Yet is this realistic? Is the problem of making policy in a highly diversified mass society really one of relating the different steps in making a decision to a single set of goals, or is it precisely one of choosing goals—of choosing goals not in the abstract, but in the convoluted context of ongoing events, with inadequate information, incomplete knowledge and understanding, and insufficient power— and doing so, in all probability, while pitted against opposition both at home and abroad? If so, the making of national decisions is not a problem for the efficiency expert or of assembling different pieces of policy logically as if the product were an automobile. Policy faces inward as much as outward, seeking to reconcile conflicting goals, to adjust aspirations to available means, and to accommodate the different advocates of these competing goals and aspirations to one another. It is here that the essence of policy making seems to lie, in a process that is in its deepest sense political.

Recognizing the political nature of policy making might help us to a better understanding of the diversity and seeming inconsistency of the goals that national policy must serve. It might also help us to understand the powerful but sometimes hidden forces through which these competing goals are reconciled, why the pushes and pulls of these crosscurrents are sometimes dampened or obscured, and why they are sometimes so fiercely public. Even the roles of such "unrational" procedures as bargaining and power might also become more clear.

President Kennedy once said, "There will always be the dark and tangled stretches in the decision-making process—mysterious even to those who may be most intimately involved. . . ."[5] Yet it is equally true that a better understanding of the process and its essentially political nature can lead to more effective policy and perhaps even to improvements in the policy-making process itself.

[5] In his foreword to Theodore C. Sorensen's *Decision-Making in the White House* (New York: Columbia University Press, 1963).

TWO
THE PRESIDENT AND
THE PRESIDENT'S MEN

A NY discussion of the making of United States foreign policy must begin with the President. It is the President to whom the Constitution assigns the task of conducting foreign affairs. It is the President who is Commander in Chief of the Armed Forces. American ambassadors overseas are not representatives of the United States, but are the personal representatives of the President himself. What is perhaps even more important than these awesome legalities, it is the President who will get the credit or the blame for whatever happens in foreign affairs. As John F. Kennedy once remarked somewhat ruefully, "The President bears the burden of the responsibility. The advisers may move on to new advice."[1]

But saying that the President is the ultimate authority in formal and legal terms and that he bears the responsibility in practical and public terms is not really saying very much. The President is only one man. Significant action on even one single problem in foreign policy—for example, ending the war in Vietnam—can occur in several places simultaneously, and the President cannot be in Washington, Saigon, and Paris at

[1] December 1962, television interview.

the same time. Being only one man, furthermore, he is also limited by time. Out of the thousands and thousands of foreign policy problems that come up each day, he can himself deal with only the most urgent, and the most urgent are not always the most important. As a consequence, the President must delegate most of the work in foreign affairs to others—to the secretary of state, and the secretary of defense, to his staff in the White House, to the under secretaries and assistant secretaries in the State Department, to the joint chiefs of staff in the Pentagon, to the director of the Central Intelligence Agency, to ambassadors overseas, and to thousands of other officials further down the line in State, Defense the CIA, and many other departments and agencies. As a result, when examining what the President does in foreign affairs, as well as what lesser officials do, it is more useful to speak not so much of his legal and formal powers, but of the role he plays in the making of foreign policy and of his power to make it.

THE PRESIDENT AS "ULTIMATE DECIDER"

The most obvious role that the President plays in the making of foreign policy is what might be called "ultimate decision maker" or "decision maker of last resort." He cannot decide on all the thousands of decisions that must be made each day, but because his is the final authority, two kinds of decisions invariably get to the top, to the President himself, either immediately and automatically or more slowly, elbowing their way past others that are also competing for a place on his crowded agenda. One is a decision that all participants recognize as fateful in the extreme. No American ambassador or American military commander in the field would take an action that he knew would run great risk of war, for example, without seeking authorization from Washington. In Washington no secretary of state or defense, no member of the joint chiefs of staff or other responsible official, military or civilian, would authorize the action without the approval of the President himself. Men do not rise to such positions without developing a sense of responsibility and integrity that would ensure that they would obtain approval for obviously fateful decisions, and even the theoretically possible exception would be restrained by his inevitable fear of certain retribution and disgrace. A decision for an act of war, a decision to commit the United States to the defense of another nation in some future set of circumstances, a decision for a major outlay of American resources, such as the Marshall Plan—all these and other similar decisions whose fateful consequences are equally obvious to everyone automatically and immediately go to the President.

The President's role as ultimate decider also makes it possible for him to take an initiative on a matter in which he has a particular and personal interest, or simply to ride his particular hobby horse. An old saying in Washington is that the head of a department can safely ignore a Presidential request the first time it is made; he can safely explain his failure to act the second time it is made; but the third time, he will have to do what the President wants. Thus on relatively minor matters, the President can almost always have his way—provided he is willing to spend the time and energy to pursue it. On grander issues, however, it is not always so, no matter how much time and energy he expends. What this power of initiative does do is to make it possible for a President to set the overall tone and thrust of the foreign policy of his administration. President Kennedy, for example, had a particular and personal interest in the developing world—Africa, Asia, and Latin America. He was not able to persuade Congress to give him anywhere near the backing he wished, but his power of initiative did enable him at least to change the emphasis and tone of United States foreign policy—through the Alliance for Progress in Latin America, his public concern with Africa, and his emphasis on development in foreign aid.

Being ultimate decider and therefore decider of last resort also ensures that another kind of decision makes its way to the President's desk—those issues over which the major departments and agencies disagree and fail to resolve their disagreement. When departments or agencies, such as State, Defense, Treasury, and the CIA disagree, or when any two of them disagree, and continue to stick stubbornly to their positions without compromise, the matter eventually must come to the President. On occasion the issue can be as lofty and fateful as that of war and peace. Every President since Roosevelt has had to deal with differences among the armed services over weapons—for example, the B-36, the Polaris submarine, TFX, and ABM—and in every case there was at least the potential of fatefulness, even if the continual bickering brought the President to exasperation. But sometimes the disagreements the President must resolve can be downright petty. President Kennedy, for example, once had to settle a dispute between the State Department and the office responsible for the Alliance for Progress over who would have priority in hiring typists.

THE PRESIDENT AS "ULTIMATE COORDINATOR"

Similar to the role of ultimate decider is the role of managerial oversight, what might be called the role of "ultimate coordinator." Once a policy is set, the departments and agencies involved in implementing the policy can be counted on to accomplish the vast bulk of the necessary coordination through simply cooperating with one another. But as with disagreement over issues, there can be disagreement in coordination, and there can also be simple failures and gaps. Ultimately it is the President who must prod and push to make sure that everyone is doing what he should. As a practical matter, the way most Presidents accomplish this managerial function is to ask the White House staff for reports on progress and status, to use the staff to follow up on decisions. In practice, in other words, the role of ultimate coordinator is exercised by the *Presidency* rather than the President himself. But on occasion the President is not content to leave the job to his staff. During the Cuban missile crisis, for example, President Kennedy personally checked on every detail, including the location of individual ships forming the blockade. During one stage of the Vietnam war, President Johnson personally passed on every target of the bombing program in North Vietnam.

THE PRESIDENT AS "ULTIMATE PERSUADER"

The President's third role in the making of foreign policy is that of principal public defender and spokesman and ultimate persuader and consensus builder. Some of this activity is very public. On many questions of foreign policy, those requiring sacrifice, for example, or having the potential for affecting the security and future of the nation, the President will present the case and do his persuading at a press conference, on a television report to the nation, or in a State of the Union message to Congress. On other occasions it is very private—when the President calls the congressional leaders to his office in an attempt to enlist their support, when he meets with the leaders of industry or labor or with the representatives of other interest groups, or when he sits through long meetings of, say, the National Security Council while the proponents of different views argue it out, ostensibly to convince him, but more often to try to persuade one another.

In the making of foreign policy, it is in these three roles that the President spends the bulk of his time. He may think about the problems of foreign policy often and more or less frequently (depending on his individual talents) come up with a creative and original idea. But no matter how successful he may be, such activity is bound to be intermittent, for his role is not that of a planner of foreign policy. Neither is his role that of chief negotiator. He may spend what seems a disproportionate amount of his time seeing high-level foreign visitors in Washington, and he may go abroad, as several recent Presidents have done for visits or for a summit meeting with the chief of state of the Soviet Union or other great powers. But although they are often useful in ratifying agreements worked out by lesser officials or in giving a President an opportunity to make some personal judgment about the men who head other nations, these visits are usually more ceremonial than functional. Certainly no President has seen his job as being that of chief negotiator since Woodrow Wilson went to Paris for the negotiations on the Treaty of Versailles.

THE PRESIDENT'S POWER

If these are the roles the President plays in the making of foreign policy, what of his power—his power to make decisions, his power to impose his *own* preferences on policy, whether for goals or means, and his power to implement his decisions?

For their part, when they look out from the White House, Presidents seem to see mostly restraints on their power. They see obstacles and opposition, whether actual or potential, in the mass publics, in the press, in the Congress, in the departments and agencies of the Executive branch, in the embassies overseas, and in the foreign governments.

The President and the mass publics

For the mass public and electorate, foreign policy is seldom a central concern. They recognize its importance, however, and the President must take care to preserve a reputation for being knowledgeable and effective in foreign affairs. This means not only that his policies must be generally successful, but that he must make the considerable effort to explain and defend his policies before the mass public, for there is always the potential for direct opposition. The possibility always exists that one of his major policies will go very wrong and impinge so heavily on the lives of ordinary people over such a long period of time that the mass public will be aroused into opposition. Vietnam is the outstanding example. When President Johnson decided in 1965 to bomb North Vietnam and send in American combat troops, there was a small group of vocal "doves" in the general public who opposed the move and a small group of vocal "hawks" who wanted the President to take even greater measures. But the vast majority of the mass public simply went along, presumably on the grounds that the President knew or ought to know best. The policy did not work, the war dragged on, the casualties mounted, and the question of the morality of our position loomed larger. Gradually public confidence in the President's policy and in the man himself eroded; gradually the number of active dissenters grew, and those dissenting increasingly came from the center as well as from the left of the political spectrum, gradually making dissent more "respectable." Eventually President Johnson was forced not only to change his policy on Vietnam, but to withdraw from the 1968 election.

The President and the press

When he looks at the press, the President sees much the same obstacle. The columnists and editorial writers help to shape opinion directly by what they write, but equally important is how the ordinary reporters and editors "play" the news. If they write from a basis of confidence in the President, some aspects of the news will receive prominence in their stories; if they write from a basis of distrust and suspiciousness, other aspects will come to the fore. Both the news interpretation by editorial writers and columnists and the news play in the straight reporting will affect opinion and behavior in the mass publics, in the Congress, and even down the line in the Executive branch itself, affecting how well and effectively the President's policies are carried out.

The President and the Congress

In the Congress, the power the President sees to restrain, block, or change his policies is more direct. Many policies, such as those relating to foreign aid, require the appropriation of money by the Congress. Others require the ratification of a treaty or the confirmation of an individual as secretary, assistant secretary, or ambassador. Still others are subject to congressional oversight. The Fulbright hearings reviewing the circumstances of the incident that led to the Tonkin Gulf resolution did much to erode confidence in the Johnson Administration's policies in Vietnam. The hearings reviewing the Johnson Administration's intervention in the Dominican Republic in 1965 were equally damaging. All policies on every conceivable issue are vulnerable to attack in speeches by individual congressmen, which in turn affects the opinions and voting behavior of other congressmen and the public at large. The congressman, in effect, competes with the President in consensus building. Even when Congress does not have direct power over a policy in the sense of being able to vote against it by rejecting a treaty or denying an appropriation, if it gets incensed enough it can adopt an obstructionist posture on things over which it does have direct power. The Congress could not force Lyndon Johnson to stop the bombing of North Vietnam and open negotiations to end the war, but by the spring of 1968, it was beginning to use its power to obstruct other matters as an *indirect* way of applying pressure on his Vietnam policy.

The President and the Executive branch

When he looks at the departments and agencies of the governments and the embassies overseas, the President sees two potential obstacles—men with some measure of power in their own right who may have policy preferences different from his, and men down the line who have little power but whose cooperation he needs if his policy is to be successfully carried out. A secretary of state, a secretary of defense, a chief of staff of the Army, or an ambassador is appointed by the President. But the fact that the man appointed is responsible for the duties of the office and that he is presumably an authority on that subject matter means that the general public, the press, and the Congress all expect that he will be heard in the councils of government. If word gets out that the President does not listen to advice from the secretary of state, the chief of staff of the Army, or other top official on matters for which they are responsible, or that the President consistently goes against their advice, questions may arise in the minds of congressmen and the general public about the President's *own* abilities and effectiveness. They may then be encouraged to use *their* power in opposition on still other matters. It is no accident that a President who has strong policy preferences usually feels compelled to try to persuade his Cabinet ministers, generals, and ambassadors of the correctness and wisdom of his preferences rather than merely command that they be obeyed. Similarly, a President who is sensitive to the fact that the success of his policy depends on how enthusiastically it is implemented will take care to do what he can to enlist support of people down the line.

The power of the President, in sum, cannot be described in a simple formula. His power is great on some issues at certain times in certain circumstances and rather small on other issues at other times in other circumstances. If the issue is one of deeply ingrained cultural attitudes, for example, the power of the President—or the chief of state in any democracy—is little more than the power to try to persuade. Alexis de Tocqueville made the point long ago when he predicted that racial prejudice in the United States would actually increase after the abolition of slavery and that this was made even more certain by the fact that the United States was a democracy. "An isolated individual," he wrote in 1830, "may surmount the prejudices of his religion, of his country, or of his race; and if this individual is a king, he may effect surprising changes in society; but a whole people cannot rise, as it were, above itself." The only thing that mitigates this harsh judgment is the fact that the Presidency, as Teddy Roosevelt remarked, is a "bully pulpit" from which to try to persuade.

In policies that require legislation, the President is somewhat better off. Although persuasion is the major power at his disposal, he also has some others when he deals with Congress. There are political favors over which he has control, and he can grant or withhold support for other policies that a reluctant congressman particularly wants. For most such policies, which include almost all domestic issues and such foreign policy issues as foreign aid, the best that can be said is that the President's power is spotty, varying widely with the circumstances and with the effort that he puts into building a consensus and gaining allies.

In foreign policy, however, except for foreign aid, the President's power is generally greater, and it increases as the issues of national security, of war and peace, become more central. President Truman decided to use American forces to resist the Communist invasion of South Korea without either a declaration of war by the Congress or even a resolution of support. President Johnson, on the other hand, did ask from Congress and receive the Tonkin Gulf resolution, which he later interpreted as authorization for his decisions in 1965 that made Vietnam an American war. Many senators vehemently disputed the interpretation Johnson gave to the Tonkin Gulf resolution, but all agreed that in making the decisions, the President was within his constitutional powers in deciding to bomb North Vietnam and that he would have been even if there had been no resolution at all.

Even the power of the purse, which the founding fathers counted on to be an effective check on the powers of the President in so many areas, is not a practical limit on the President in time of war, even limited war. A congressman is too vulnerable to the political charge that he is taking the weapons and ammunition out of the hands of men already being shot at. That the congressman thinks the particular war is wrong does not justify a vote that deprives the men in the field of the means to defend themselves. Of the two or three dozen senators who opposed the war in the period between 1965 and 1968, only Senator Gruening of Alaska and Senator Morse of Oregon actually voted against the military appropriations bill that provided the money for the war, and it is probably not unrelated that both were defeated in 1968 even though antiwar sentiment was stronger then than ever before.

Presidential power in foreign affairs

In a sense the reason the President's power in the field of foreign affairs increases as the issues of war and peace become more central is that from both constitutional and practical considerations he is freer on such issues from the oversight and control of both Congress and the general public. Everyone recognizes that in times of peril the President may have to act quickly and often secretly and that there might be neither time nor appropriate opportunity for the open and lengthy procedures by which Congress and the public could be brought into the decision. Congressmen themselves are disposed to take this stand and to point to the Cuban missile crisis as an example. The Soviet missiles were discovered on October 14. If it was to be effective, action had to be taken before they became operational, which was about October 26th in the case of the medium-range missiles and would have been sometime in November in the case of the intermediate-range missiles. This meant that President Kennedy had only a week or so to explore the alternatives and decide what to do, and it had to be done in secrecy. Most congressmen feel that there is simply no practical way that Congress could be brought into such a decision.

Just because the Congress and the general public cannot effectively participate in such decisions and the President is consequently more powerful does not mean that he is all-powerful. For any major decision, he must have the support or at least the passive acquiescence of most and sometimes all of the principal officers in the Executive branch.

Changing an on-going policy is particularly difficult, even in these areas where the President's power is the greatest. When President Kennedy came into office, for example, Laos was the most difficult and urgent problem facing him. The existing policy inherited from the Eisenhower Administration was to support the right-wing faction in Laos with arms aid in fighting the Communist and neutralist factions. The Eisenhower policy also included rejection of both the alternative of escalating the struggle by introducing American bombers or ground forces and the alternative of negotiating a compromise settlement that would lead to a neutralized Laos in which the Communists would participate in a coalition government headed by the neutralists. Both in the Eisenhower

Administration and in the early part of the Kennedy Administration, attempts were made in one or another part of the government to change the policy and adopt one or another alternative, but they came to nothing. Each time, those who wanted to escalate the war were opposed by those who wanted to negotiate a compromise settlement, and it was a third faction who prevailed—those who wanted to continue the existing policy.

The President's power in a crisis

In general terms the argument that a little more time is needed to provide a fair test of the present policy, whatever it may be, is very often persuasive. Every alternative has its risks and uncertainties, and no one can be quite sure that some bold new departure will not lead to an awesome new disaster. Indeed, even in those issues of war and peace where his power is greatest, the President is usually not free to effect drastic changes in an on-going policy until there is a crisis—a crisis defined as a situation in which all the major participants agree that continuing the present policy will certainly bring failure as great as the potential failure of the possible alternative policies. The crisis came in Laos in early 1961, when all the major participants—from the Pentagon, the State Department, the CIA, and the White House—agreed that the policy of supporting the right-wing faction was hopeless. There were opposing factions, one advocating escalation and the other negotiation, which were rather evenly balanced, and President Kennedy was therefore free not only to change existing policy, but to choose between the two major alternatives. He chose to negotiate, and this led to the neutralization of Laos by the Geneva agreements of 1962.

President Johnson and Vietnam

A similar situation prevailed in the Johnson Administration over policy toward Vietnam. When he assumed the Presidency in late 1963 following the assassination of President Kennedy,

President Johnson inherited a policy that had been started by President Eisenhower and continued by Kennedy, that of supporting the South Vietnamese government with American aid and a limited number of advisers. It is clear that President Johnson felt more strongly than Kennedy that American security was affected by the struggle in Vietnam.[1] But even if he had wanted to make a drastic change before he was himself convinced that the existing policy was doomed to failure, it is doubtful whether he could have brought it off. Once again it was only when the crisis came in December 1964 and January 1965 and all the major participants agreed that continuing existing policy would not work that a major change in policy became politically possible. Once again the "hawk" faction advocating an escalation of the war was balanced by a "dove" faction advocating negotiations, and the President was relatively free. In the end President Johnson went in the opposite direction from what Kennedy did in Laos, deciding first to bomb North Vietnam and a few weeks later to send American ground forces.

In these two examples, circumstances conspired to maximize the President's power. The fact of a crisis made a drastic change politically possible, and the roughly balanced power of the factions advocating different policies left the President relatively free of any pressures besides his own personal preferences and convictions.

President Eisenhower and Dienbienphu

It is not always so, however, even in circumstances that appear to be highly similar. Consider the situation facing President Eisenhower in Vietnam in 1954, at the time of the battle of Dienbienphu.[2] The French had been fighting the Viet Minh,

---

[1] For an analysis of the evidence supporting this conclusion, see the paperback edition of my To Move a Nation, chap. 34, and the long footnote on page 537, which was added after publication of the hardcover edition.
[2] The following account is drawn from Melvin Gurtov, The First Vietnam Crisis (New York, 1967).

led by Ho Chi Minh and the Communist party of Vietnam. Existing American policy was to support the French with, again, arms and equipment, but to reject the alternatives either of using American combat troops or of working for a negotiated settlement. The crisis was the battle of Dienbien-phu and the imminent collapse of the French military effort. Very powerful forces within the Eisenhower Administration favored an American intervention—Vice President Richard M. Nixon, the Secretary of State, John Foster Dulles, and the Chairman of the Joint Chiefs of Staff, Admiral Arthur W. Rad-ford. There were also "doves" who were reluctant to see American forces used in Vietnam. The most powerful of these were the Congressional leadership among whom, iron-ically in view of what happened in 1965, was Lyndon B. John-son, the Majority Leader. In essence the congressional leaders were not willing to support an American intervention unless our European allies, principally Great Britain, agreed to go into Vietnam with us. The British said no.

Thus the situation in 1954 was apparently identical to the situation President Kennedy faced in 1961 in Laos and the situation President Johnson faced in 1965 in Vietnam—a crisis in which all agreed that the existing policy would no longer work, and a rough balance between "hawks" and "doves" leaving the President relatively free to choose. In fact, how-ever, in 1954 there was one additional opponent to the policy of intervention who occupied a position that as a practical, political matter virtually gave him a veto. The man was General Matthew B. Ridgway, Chief of Staff of the United States Army.

General Ridgway was convinced that an American inter-vention would be a mistake. He sent a team of experts to Viet-nam to look at the situation and then prepared a report for the President arguing that bombing would not work in Viet-nam, that if the United States decided on bombing it would have to follow up with a total of at least six Army divisions, and that because the terrain in Vietnam was so ideal for guerrillas the American force could expect very heavy casualties. The implication was that even six divisions might not succeed.

As a result President Eisenhower was not as free as Kennedy and Johnson found themselves to be. A President whose military advisers are "hawks" and whose civilian advisers are "doves" can decide pretty much as he chooses, but any President, even a former five-star general, would be very, very hesitant in deciding on a military intervention that the chief of staff of the Army insisted would be a military disaster. If the adventure failed, the fact that the Army chief of staff had objected to it would inevitably become known, and the political consequences for the President, for his administration, for his party, and for his place in history would be overwhelming.

The power of the President, in sum, is vast, but it is not so much the power to command as the power to lead, to persuade, to bargain and maneuver in the building of a consensus. It is this central fact that President Truman had in mind when he chuckled over the difficulties he foresaw for President Eisenhower. It was also this central fact that Kennedy had in mind when he spoke of the "inner club" and their trials and tribulations in attempting to keep the government together and all the different participants "on board." And it was this central fact that Neustadt had in mind when he spoke of the "half-observed realities of Presidents-in-sneakers, stirrups in hand, trying to induce" so many different power holders to go along.

OTHER MEMBERS OF AN ADMINISTRATION

What of the roles and powers of the other members of the Executive branch? The first to consider is the group of men and women who collectively constitute what people mean when they speak of an "administration"—the secretaries of the major departments, the under secretaries and assistant secretaries, the White House staff, and the directors of such agencies as the Central Intelligence Agency and the Agency for International Development. Roughly speaking, an administration consists of Presidential appointees and the people that Presidential appointees in turn choose as their immediate staff.

An obvious function of these people who make up an administration is to be the President's men, the representatives of the administration. If a Presidential appointee is in a staff job in the White House, this is the total of his function. He is expected to jab and prod and push all the different bureaucracies. He must make sure that they produce the data, analyses, and recommendations that the President needs in order to make decisions. He must follow up on decisions to make sure that the bureaucracies take timely and effective action in carrying them out once they are made.

The Presidential appointee who heads a department, agency, or bureau or who serves in a line job in one of them—a secretary, director, or assistant secretary—is expected to shape and mold the bureaucracy to the President's needs. He must represent political management, represent the top level of the administration in the form either of the President or of the Cabinet member in whose department he serves. But if he is the President's man with the careerists, the Presidential appointee in the line job should also be the careerists' man with the President. He should represent the specialists' view to the President and his Cabinet officers and be the vehicle for their expertise. He must be the judge of whether what they have to say should be laid before the highest councils, but when he does decide that their views should be heard, he ought to be their unrelenting champion. The head of a department, bureau, or agency and the Presidential appointees who serve in them *should* run interference for their organization and its careerists. Otherwise, in a political process of decision making, their expertise will go unheard.

The assistant secretaries

All this applies to the Cabinet member—the secretary heading a department or the director of an independent agency.

It also applies in general to lower ranking Presidential appointees. Some of these, in fact, may have a relationship to the President almost exactly similar to that of a Cabinet member. In the Kennedy Administration, for example, G. Mennen Williams enjoyed this status as Assistant Secretary for African Affairs. Williams had served several terms as Governor of Michigan and wielded political power in his own right, both as a former governor and as a spokesman for the liberal wing of the Democratic party. At the same time, President Kennedy was deeply interested in the problems of Africa and had confidence in Williams as Assistant Secretary. As a result Williams had a special status and a special relationship to both the President and the Secretary of State. On the other hand, the position of the Assistant Secretary for Near Eastern and South Asian Affairs, held by Phillips Talbot in the Kennedy Administration, was less independent, more closely tied to the position of the Secretary of State than to the President.

In general, however, most assistant secretaries occupy a position between these two extremes typified by Williams and Talbot, although their *function* is essentially the same. There are five regional assistant secretaries of state—African affairs, European affairs, Latin American affairs, East Asian and Pacific affairs, and Near Eastern and South Asian affairs—and the job is, in the words of former Secretary of State Dean Rusk, "the crucial post in terms of the art of management of policy in our relations with the rest of the world."[3]

The reasons that the post of regional assistant secretary is crucial are both human and political. The secretary of state can give very broad guidance over the whole range of foreign policy, as well as leadership. He can also manage a particular crisis, if he has the specialized knowledge and the desire to do it, as Secretary Dulles, for example, personally managed the Quemoy-Matsu crisis of 1958. As a practical matter, too, secretaries of state have also taken over the day-by-day management of two or three of the most important continuing

[3] In his testimony before the Jackson Subcommittee on December 11, 1963.

problems. In the post-World War II world, for example, most secretaries of state have for obvious reasons made relations with the Soviet Union their principal concern, as well as the concomitant liaison with the United Kingdom, France, and Germany. But the foreign affairs of a great power are too extensive for one man to manage them all, and for this very human reason the secretary must delegate responsibility for managing relations with most of the world to other men.

For political reasons there is also a limit on how far down the line this delegation of responsibilities can go. Significant items of foreign policy cannot be managed at a level lower than a member of the administration, a man who is appointed by the President and who is therefore in a position at least to begin to inject into policy the broad political considerations that must peculiarly concern the President. What this entails are such considerations as the effect of foreign policy on different segments of American society and the special interest groups that are affected; what the Congress, the press, and the mass of the people will accept; and how much effort will have to be made to develop the kind of consensus and public support that will be needed. Only the President can apply this kind of broad political judgment to policy in any final sense, but each of the five regional assistant secretaries is important precisely because he is the President's appointee, and as such is the junction at which all strands of policy—political, military, economic, and diplomatic—first come together. His is the *first* level in government that can begin to apply these broad political considerations to policy and the management of foreign affairs. As Paul H. Nitze once remarked, the regional assistant secretary is the first person on the ladder who can *commit* the United States of America.

Since it is the function of a Presidential appointee to represent the men and women who make up the organizations they head, it is not surprising that they frequently come to identify themselves with these organizations and to defend the organizational view with great passion. This is, obviously, one source of the tension between Presidents and Cabinet officers that has been so often remarked upon. It is also another reason why Presidents must go consensus building in the Executive branch as well as in the wider rings of policy making.

Occasionally a Presidential appointee also has the function of representing an outside, public constituency. President Kennedy chose Mennen Williams for the Africa post, for example, because he represented liberal opinion in the United States. He chose Adlai Stevenson to be the United States Ambassador to the United Nations for the same reason. He chose John McCone—an Irish Catholic, a Republican, and a millionaire ship-building tycoon—to head the CIA precisely because he wanted to make the conservatives in business, in industry, in the military, and in Congress feel that they and their foreign and defense policy interests would be represented. Thus the function of these men in the President's mind was to represent an outside constituency. In this, of course, is another source of tension. Having chosen men because of their affiliations with particular constituencies, a President can hardly be surprised if they speak for that constituency in the internal policy debate.

The "front men"

The function of these men, in sum, is to be the advocates of policy and to represent the different bureaucratic constituencies inside the government and the public constituencies, special interests, and attentive publics outside the government. It is their function to force an issue to decision, to try to make the government face up to an emerging problem. It is their function to put forward an alternative policy and to become identified with it. They are the "front men." If they are not already public figures, they will be soon.

A front man need not be a specialist in a particular subject, but if he lasts, he is or will become a specialist in using specialists, in knowing when the specialists are right and should be backed and when they are caught up in their own parochialism. It is the front man who pushes for a particular policy at different places inside the government and outside, with higher officials and lower, with other agencies, in congressional hearings, in backgrounders with the press, in public speeches, and in endless struggles over countless pieces of paper. It is the front man who is the leader of a constituency, the sponsor of a policy, and the principle builder of a consensus for it. Career men down the line may push a particular policy with unrelenting passion, they may be advocates to the core fiber of their beings, but it is this front man who is *the* advocate. The *function* of advocacy is his. He is the man who runs interference by the nature of his job. Out ahead, as he is, he is the one who first feels the blast of political heat—and this, too, is part of his function.

The power of the front men

What is the power of the front man? The secretary of state or defense, an assistant secretary, or any Presidential appointee who heads a particular bureaucracy has the power at the very minimum to cause papers to be written, information to be amassed, and recommendations to be made. He who commands bureaucracy controls the power to table papers. At meetings where many different organizations are represented, he who has the power to table papers commands the frame of reference of the discussion and in many cases can dominate the final decision itself—for it is only when the issue cuts deeply into the interests of the other organizations that they will be able to find the time to develop position papers of their own. The head of a bureaucracy has power by virtue of his day-to-day direction of the activities of the bureaucracy, in terms not only of the problems he will study, but of the manner in which he carries out policy, indifferently or energetically.

A secretary or an assistant secretary has some power by virtue of the *authority* of the office he holds, even though he was appointed to that office by the President and continues to hold it only at the pleasure of the President. The appointee has at least the right to be heard and the power to be persuasive—for if, as already mentioned, word gets out that the

President does not listen to advice from the official responsible for the particular matter, the fact that he does not listen may backfire on the President himself. On very specific matters carrying the presumption of a special expertise, the power of the front man may be very great at least in terms of being able to block action. The best example is probably the one already given—General Ridgway's successful attempt to block the decision to intervene with American troops in Vietnam.

Thus at one extreme, the front man, once appointed, always carries the implicit threat that he might resign with a public blast if the President goes directly against his advice or refuses even to let him be heard—but that is a card that can be played only once. At the other extreme is the front man who holds not only the office but enjoys the confidence of the President in his subject field—and that man has power that is enormous.

THREE
THE CAREER BUREAUCRATS:
CIVILIAN AND MILITARY

AT the next level in the Executive branch, below the front men of a particular administration, are the career civil servants in the various departments and the officer corps of the military services. Probably the first thing that must be said in analyzing the roles and functions they perform is that a distinction must be made between the role and power of career officials acting as individuals and the role and power of career officials acting collectively as organizations.

As individuals the military officer and career civil servant perform similar functions. They serve as technical experts in the amassing of information and the exploration of policy recommendations and as day-to-day managers in the carrying out of policy in their field of responsibility. The power that they exercise can vary enormously. The power of a chief of staff of the Army, like General Ridgway, or a commander in the field, like General Westmoreland in Vietnam, is really as great as that of a front man, a secretary or assistant secretary of state or defense. Even down the line in a bureaucracy, the power of an individual who possesses a public reputation can be very great in the field of his specialty. When Wolf Ladejinsky, who is among the world's foremost authorities on land reform, was the chief adviser on such matters in the Agency for International Development, for example, even the President would have found it difficult to tamper with the details of the programs he designed.

Even the less famous official can have considerable influence, at least over the narrow range of his immediate responsibilities. In the amassing of information and the making of recommendations, he has the power to persuade by the way he presents the information and the skill with which he argues his case. In the implementing stage, also, he can often make or break a policy by the vigor with which he carries it out, not to mention the possibility of skewing a policy in one direction or the other by the way that it is implemented.

All this seems to give even the relatively obscure and minor individual official considerable power, but it is less than it seems. In the first place, the individual officer's purview and hence his power is over a very narrow range of policy, and he is usually concerned more with the technical aspects of policy than with its overall direction. He has almost no power beyond that narrow and technical range of policy for which he is directly responsible. In the second place, the individual official is subject to supervision by higher officials right up to the front men of the administration who can reverse his action or remove him if he consistently and blatantly imposes his own views and preferences on policy. The best example of this is not that of an obscure official but a very famous one—General MacArthur. During the Korean War, when he was Commander of all the American forces, General MacArthur made public statements threatening Communist China with air attacks, which was against the President's policy. To make matters worse, the General did not clear his statements with Washington, as he had been instructed to do. President Truman, quite simply, fired him. The point is that if it can happen to someone as famous as General MacArthur, it can surely happen to others who are not famous at all.

ORGANIZATIONS AS ORGANIZATIONS

All this applies to the *individual* civil servant or military officer. When the bureaucracy, civil or military, is considered as an organization, however, both roles and powers are different.

Organizations have interests of their own that are sometimes more than the sum of the interests of the individual members of the organization. The United States Cavalry, for example, was an organization dedicated to the use of the horse in warfare. The Cavalry continued to buy and train horses and to fight to protect the role and mission of the Cavalry in competition with other services long after most of the individual members of the Cavalry had ceased to believe that the horse had any importance in the future war.[1] Similarly, the United States Air Force is an organization dedicated to the use of the manned bomber in warfare, and as an organization it may continue to fight for the role of the manned bomber past the time when objective outsiders consider the bomber useful. At the very least, one might say that to understand all the nuances of, say, United States bombing policy in the Vietnam War, it is probably necessary also to understand the peculiar stake that the Air Force has as an organization.

This is not meant to imply that organizations in some mystical way have minds and wills of their own. Part of the reason for the slow demise of the Cavalry was sentiment, rationalization, and all the other perfectly human failings of the men concerned, but part of it was something else. The job of the chief of Cavalry and the other officers with him was this particular aspect of warfare. Even though they might have personal doubts about the future of the horse in warfare, providing for that potential aspect of warfare was their job, that was what they continued to do and were expected to continue to do. To do anything less would be to raise questions about their

[1] Edward L. Katzenbach, Jr., "The Horse Cavalry in the Twentieth Century: A Study on Policy Response," *Public Policy* (Cambridge, Mass.: Graduate School of Public Administration, Harvard University, 1958).

fitness for any job. The specialization of function that is the essence of bureaucracy, civilian or military, will ensure that officials who belong to those organizations will behave in ways that appear to give organizations interests and policy convictions beyond the interests and policy convictions of the men and women who make up the organization.

Dozens, perhaps hundreds, of governmental organizations or bureaucracies that have some influence on foreign policy exist, ranging from the Immigration Service and the Peace Corps to the Commerce Department and Treasury. But three deserve special attention here—the State Department, the military services, and the Central Intelligence Agency.

The Department of State

Prior to World War II, the United States did not think of itself as a global power, and its State Department reflected that attitude. The whole department along with the top echelons of both the War and Navy Departments was comfortably housed in what is now known as the Executive Office Building, while the foreign service representatives abroad numbered fewer than 2,000. Today the department occupies not one but several buildings the size of the old State-War-Navy building, and the total personnel overseas numbers more than 34,000.

Prior to World War II, the posts in Washington were manned largely by civil servants and those overseas by members of the foreign service. Then in 1954, as a result of the so-called Wriston report, the departmental service was very largely incorporated into the foreign service. Today, except for certain jobs calling for a very high degree of specialization, most positions both in Washington and abroad are filled by officers of the foreign service.

Like the officer corps of the military services, the foreign service is a career service. Except for rare and exceptional cases of "lateral entry" into the service, officers are recruited shortly after they finish college by means of a rigorous series of written and oral examinations, and work their way up through the ranks.

Organization of the Department of State

Although it is often hard to convince the skeptical outsider, the organization of the Department of State is not complicated. At the top is the secretary of state and the under secretary, who acts as his deputy. A second under secretary has at different times specialized in economic affairs or political affairs, reflecting either the interests of the incumbent at the time or the relative balance of power among the top echelons. A fourth position is that of deputy under secretary for political affairs. The title is misleading, for he has never served as a true deputy. Traditionally this position has been reserved for a career foreign service officer, although the incumbent is a Presidential appointee and must be confirmed by the Senate. As things have evolved, the deputy under secretary has been responsible for all matters involving both the military and the intelligence agencies. There is also a deputy under secretary for administration, who is not concerned with policy, but with logistics and personnel—everything from promotion and assignments to communications, office space, and travel allowances. In recent years there has also been a counsellor of the state department and a special assistant with rank of ambassador. The special assistant has been one of the top career foreign service officers specializing in the Soviet Union—in every case a former ambassador to that country—and his responsibility has been to advise on matters pertaining to relations with the Soviets in all respects. The other job, that of counsellor, has been somewhat ambiguous. It ranks high in terms of protocol, and its incumbent has occasionally been charged with important responsibilities of various kinds. Just as often, however, it has been a position to which a man can be gracefully "kicked upstairs."

All these men in the very top echelon of the department have private secretaries and stenographers and one, two, or even three special assistants who help in everything from writing speeches to following up on decisions already made. The deputy under secretary for political affairs also has a small staff section to deal with politico-miiltary affairs that tend to cut across regional lines. Except for the secretary of state himself, who of course heads the whole department, none of these officers heads a bureaucracy.

The five regional assistant secretaries come next—European affairs, East Asian and Pacific affairs, African affairs, Latin American affairs, and Near Eastern and South Asian affairs. Unlike the officers at the top echelon, each of the assistant secretaries does head a bureaucracy—the Bureau of European Affairs, the Bureau of African Affairs, and so on. In the past the bureaus were further subdivided into offices, each of which dealt with a smaller group of countries. The Office of East Asian Affairs, for example, dealt with China, Korea, and Japan. Then came the "country desk"—one or several officers dealing with a particular country, such as Japan. Recently the department has been experimenting with upgrading the country desk by making the head of it a man of higher rank than in the past and eliminating the "office" level entirely. In some cases, however, the office level has reappeared in the guise of a deputy assistant secretary concentrating on a small group of countries, just as the office director did before.

In addition there are a number of functional bureaus, each headed by an assistant secretary—the Bureau of Congressional Relations, Economic Affairs, International Organization Affairs, Intelligence and Research, Public Affairs, the Legal Adviser, Educational and Cultural Affairs, and Protocol. One other assistant secretary heads the small Policy Planning staff. Still another bureau, that of Security and Consular Affairs, which handles such things as passports and visas, is headed by a director.

Criticisms of the State Department

Two criticisms of the State Department and the foreign service have been most persistent, one emanating most frequently from Congress and the other from the White House.

In Congress the fear is that the foreign service is manned not by typical Americans but by "striped-pants cookie pushers"—socialites from effete, Eastern seaboard, upper class families—and that their long service abroad leads them to become too cosmopolitan to represent the United States effectively. The fear has been sufficiently pervasive to have influenced legislation regulating the foreign service on many occasions. The most obvious example, which happens to be very beneficial for a variety of other reasons, is the provision in the law that foreign service officers must serve a certain proportion of their time in the United States and that they must be brought back for a period of home leave every two years.

Before World War II, the notion that foreign service officers were mainly upper class had some basis in fact. It was a very small corps with very few opportunities for training in language, and the salaries and allowances were grossly inadequate. The men and women attracted to the service tended to be those who already had special training or who had already lived abroad in their childhood and who had some private income to supplement the meager salaries.

Since World War II, however, the foreign service has been fundamentally changed. The Wriston program brought in a large number of officers of diverse background. The recruitment program has cast a much wider net than in the past. The pay and allowances have been made competitive with other professional careers, the Foreign Service Institute provides language and other kinds of training, and money is also available for mid-career training of all kinds at various universities across the country. Today the foreign service is as much a cross section of American society as any other profession.

As for the fear that foreign service officers who spend long years abroad will become so cosmopolitan that they can no longer represent the United States effectively, it is, of course, true that a man who has spent considerable time in a particular country develops a special understanding of its peculiar problems and frequently a fondness for its people. The foreign service itself jokingly refers to the tendency as a malady, "localitis." But a special understanding of the problems of a particular country and even a special fondness for its people are obviously not necessarily a liability for a man representing the United States. More often it is an asset.

The second persistent criticism of the State Department and the Foreign Service, emanating most frequently from the White House, is more real. President Kennedy, for example, once called the State Department a "bowl full of jelly." His criticism is one that most Presidents and their immediate White House aides have made, that the State Department is slow in acting, requiring endless "clearances" from the different bureaus and offices before taking an action; that it is frequently indecisive in the actions it does take; and that it often fails to provide the strong overall leadership to the other departments and agencies that is needed if United States foreign policy is to be effective and consistent.

The charge, unfortunately, is not completely unfair. The State Department is slow and it does often fail to provide strong leadership. Some of the blame undoubtedly belongs to the department, but some of it is inherent in the nature of the work the department is called upon to do. There are reasons for its failures, in other words, that are not always the fault of the State Department.

The power of the State Department

In the first place, the State Department, unlike all its rival departments and agencies in the government, has no natural constituency in the broad public and few natural allies in industry, the press, and the Congress. The Pentagon has as a general constituency the veterans organizations, the reserve and national guard organizations, and a great variety of patriotic societies. The purpose of the military is to smite our enemies, not to negotiate with them, and the Pentagon can appeal to a very broad constituency as the champion of right and the protector of flag, country, and motherhood. The State Department, on the other hand, has neither natural constituency nor broad appeal. It is responsible for dealing with foreigners, and, unfortunately for the State Department, foreigners do not vote in American elections.

Beyond its broad and general constituency, the Pentagon also has natural allies who are extremely powerful in their own right, while the State Department has none. The total State Department budget in recent years has been in the neighborhood of 350 million dollars, most of which goes for salaries. The budget of the Pentagon, on the other hand, has been running between 70 and 80 *billion* dollars, most of which goes for the purchase of hardware—tanks, guns, airplanes, trucks, electronic equipment, and so on. It is no accident that the military have sympathetic friends and natural allies in the most powerful segments of industry and also among the senators and congressmen who represent the states in which that industry is located. Without either a general constituency or natural allies in industry and Congress, the State Department lacks the power to exercise the strong and vigorous leadership demanded of it.

If the lack of a constituency and of natural allies were not enough, the State Department is further weakened by the very nature of foreign affairs. It must deal with over 125 nations, with various regions, and a variety of international organizations. Each of these has its own rivalries and clashing interests with the others. Inevitably these clashing interests are reflected in the State Department itself. It is only natural that men dealing with particular nations and problems would prefer to see the United States adopt policies that help improve relations with the states for which they are responsible or that tend to solve the problems with which they must deal. The trouble is that policies that help with one nation or problem may at the same time hurt with another nation or problem. It is no accident that in the Congo crisis, for example, the State Department was divided between a "New Africa" group who wanted to pursue policies that improved relations with the newly independent states of Africa and an "Old Europe" group who opposed those policies on the ground that they hurt relations with the European countries that were trying to maintain influence in their former colonies.[2] As a result of the very nature of foreign affairs, in other words, the State Department can only rarely present a strong and unified front to the rest of the actors in the policy-making process whose interests cover a narrower and sharper range of subject matter.

The military

Since the National Security Act of 1947, which made the Air Force a separate service equal with the Army and the Navy, the dominant group in the present organization of the military services is the joint chiefs of staff, the JCS. Each of the services is headed by a chief of staff who is supported by a staff on his own as well as by the bureaucracy of the particular service. The three service chiefs together with another senior officer, the chairman of the joint chiefs, make up the JCS. It is a collegial body; the chairman has no more power than an individual chief, and as practical matter he may have less. Also as a practical matter, the JCS usually operate on the basis of unanimity, although each has a vote and at times decisions are made as a result of voting. The JCS also have a bureaucracy of their own, a group of staff officers working directly for the chiefs as a body.

Each of the services is powerful in its own right and makes decisions affecting only its own service without reference to the JCS. But when the military makes a recommendation to the President on overall military matters or when problems arise that affect more than one service, it is made through the JCS.

Each of the services also has a civilian head—the secretaries of the Army, Navy, and Air Force—and various civilian under secretaries and assistant secretaries. But since 1947 these officials have not had the power they formerly enjoyed and have had relatively little influence on policy.

The civilian officials who have had power and who have

[2] For a detailed description of the struggle between these two factions during the Congo crisis, see my *To Move a Nation*, part 4.

influenced policy in recent years are the secretary of defense, the deputy secretary of defense, the comptroller, and the assistant secretary of defense for international security affairs. In the period in which Robert S. McNamara was Secretary of Defense, these top civilians in the Pentagon exercised so much power so effectively that they engendered considerable animosity among the military. McNamara himself had had experience managing a large organization as one of the top officers of the Ford Motor Company, and he applied these methods to the Pentagon. Although James Forrestal, the first Secretary of Defense probably had more influence in the area in which defense policy and foreign policy intertwined, McNamara was the only Secretary of Defense who was able to force the bickering, rival services into line. He did it by means of a group of so-called "whiz kids" from academia and the RAND Corporation, who were either specialists on "cost effectiveness" techniques or in international affairs. The specialists on cost effectiveness worked in the office of the comptroller or in the secretary's personal office to bring some rationality into the weapons systems over which the services had been battling, and the international affairs specialists went into the Office of International Security Affairs (ISA), which was mainly responsible for matters that involved the Department of State.

Even at the height of McNamara's power and influence, the power the military continued to exercise was formidable. Both before and since McNamara, the power of the military has been even greater.

The power of the military

The problem of the military stems partly from the very fact of their power, or at least their potential power. As just described, the power available to the military in the day-by-day policy debate in Washington on matters in their field of responsibility derives in part from their wide constituency in the general electorate and their natural allies in industry, the press, and Congress. Because they exercise legal control over the ultimate means of violence available to a society, their *potential* for power is theoretically unlimited. It is for this reason that the military have been the object of suspicion and distrust, and especially so in democracies. So long as it is not a world of a single universal government and the nations must rely for their security principally on themselves, they will continue to establish armed forces for their protection against outside threats. Every democratic society faces the danger that these forces of arms and men trained in their use will be used against the society that created them. One or the other party or political faction may gain control of the army and use it to gain political power or prevent the transfer of power to rivals who have won it by constitutional means. A popular general, a "man on horseback," may use the army to put himself in control of the state. The military as a group may set itself up as a state within a state that can veto or dictate the nation's policy.

History abounds in examples of all of these. Caesar and Napoleon were both men on horseback, as Nasser has been more recently. The Bolsheviks subverted the loyalties of the naval garrison at Kronstadt to help themselves into power and have used the army against rivals even within their own party. For the state within a state, there is the classic example of the Prussian Army. Here was an officer corps that sat apart, almost disdaining direct political power, but regarding themselves as the true repository of the national ethos and not hesitating to try to dictate policy whenever they felt it in the interest of the "higher" state they saw themselves as representing.

The principle of civilian supremacy

It is these threats that the principle of civilian supremacy over the military is designed to meet. That civil power shall be supreme means only that the use of a nation's armed might shall be determined by constitutional processes. If constitutional processes are observed, a military leader cannot usurp power, no single political faction can subvert the military for its own purposes, and the military as a group will be unable to dictate policy from their essentially parochial view.

Whether a nation is successful in establishing the principle of civilian supremacy depends on many things. It depends in the first instance on the civilians. If there is to be civilian supremacy, the people must cherish their constitution and insist on rejecting any man or party who violates it, even in the name of a good cause. Secondly, success in establishing the principle of civilian supremacy also depends on the military, on whether they are loyal and conscientious civil servants and, most importantly, on whether they are woven into the fabric of national life or stand apart.

So far the United States has been fortunate in its soldiers. Now and then a military hero has become President, but the armed forces as such have never been the instrument of his gaining the White House, nor have they enjoyed any special influence after he arrived there. Sometimes it has been quite the reverse. Much to the disgust of the Army, to which Eisenhower had belonged, for example, it was the Eisenhower Administration that decided on the so-called New Look military policy that emphasized air power at the expense of the ground forces! The military has not had the determining voice on questions of when it should be used in domestic disturbances, nor has it had any compelling identification with a particular region or class. At the time of the Civil War, for example, a somewhat larger proportion of the officer corps came from the South than from any other region, but those who could not loyally support the federal government resigned. It was the individual and not the army as such that was identified with the South.

One reason the behavior of the American soldier has been so exemplary in remaining obedient to civilian control is that the officer corps has been drawn mainly from the lower middle classes. These are themselves antimilitarist, opposed to any suggestion that war is an end in itself to be gloried in, and equally opposed to the inhumanity of the martinet's love of discipline for its own sake. The officer recruit does not acquire a new basic philosophy on joining his new profession; he carries over his old one. In this respect America's good fortune has been that it had no aristocracy that could have sustained an effective effort to monopolize the officer corps. The end of the plantation system in the Civil War restricted the development of the southern aristocracy, who did indeed have a tradition of military glory; and the other potential aristocracies have largely turned to commerce and finance.

Then, too, administrative practices in the armed forces themselves have helped in avoiding ties to a particular class or region. West Point cadets are appointed to the academy by their congressmen, which guarantees a geographic spread and takes the actual recruitment decision out of the hands of the military. And not all officers are West Pointers. West Point has never provided more than about 40 percent of the officer corps, and has provided much less than that in recent times.

Undoubtedly the most important of all the reasons for the professional American soldier's respect for the principle of civilian supremacy is the long-standing tradition in the services that the officer corps should be apolitical. Their indoctrination in this tradition is both formal and informal. The point is made in the training of a young officer. But it is informally, in the endless expressions of approval and disapproval of the acts of fellow officers, superiors, and historical forerunners that the young officer builds up a set of criteria about what kinds of behavior are appropriate in what kinds of circumstances. It is a tribute to the American military that those criteria are those of the society as a whole.

The conclusion one can draw from all this is that America has no reason to fear that its military will produce a man on horseback, that the military will easily be subverted by any one political faction, or that they will attempt to set themselves up as a state within a state.

Fear of the militarization of national policy

A second criticism—or fear—of the military is more subtle. Pointing to the military's natural allies in industry, the press, and Congress already described, some critics see the military playing a much larger role in the making of our foreign policy than ever before. In time of prolonged international crisis, a very large proportion of our national substance goes into military preparedness. All around the world, the United States maintains military bases, and their mere existence affects our relations with almost every nation of any size and significance in the world. Thus the military is not only powerful, but it has a legitimate concern in almost every aspect of our foreign policy. At the same time, these critics remember with misgivings the old charges against the military of extreme conservatism, of being nationalistic and aggressive, and especially of being power oriented and simplistic, tending to meet the complex problems of diplomacy by a resort to crude force.

Many, even among ardent antimilitarists, would admit that such a picture is a stereotype, a crude exaggeration, but many also fear that it contains some truth. One has only to glance over either the popular or the scholarly literature of the past few years to see that the reality of the "military mind" has been widely accepted by responsible people. Yet one wonders whether this kind of generalization is as useful as it is dangerous.

If the American military tend to be conservative, this fact probably points to the conservatism of the lower middle classes from which they spring. Since these lower middle classes constitute the bulk of Americans, one might argue that the problem here is not so much the "military" mind as it is the middle-class American mind. When a narrow, specialized class and the profession of arms becomes one, as with the Junkers of Prussia, the goals of both will be reflected in child training, and one might be able to speak of the inevitable conservatism of a "military mind." But in a society in which the military are recruited in adulthood from a wide base, it seems doubtful that the act of putting on a uniform would make a man more sympathetic to one basic political philosophy than to another.

Monarchies, aristocracies, bourgeois democracies, Fascist and Communist dictatorships have all produced successful armies. One would therefore conclude that the military are not a thing apart, but are a reflection of the society from which they spring. It was Marx and Engels, after all, who long ago discovered that there is nothing to prevent a socialist state from having a socialist army—that there is nothing, indeed, to prevent an army from becoming an instrument for creating the socialist state.

As for intellectual rigidity, an excessive emphasis on discipline, and other such personal qualities attributed to the military, it does indeed seem reasonable to suppose that practicing the military art would encourage a man to develop in himself qualities of decisiveness, energy, loyalty to the decisions of higher authority, disciplined teamwork, and the other virtues necessary to large organizations engaged in implementing, rather than evolving, ideas, policies, and programs. By this very concentration, the soldier would tend to neglect the virtues of the thinker and writer—subtlety, qualification, and habits of probing the assumptions behind goals and ways of life.

How in this respect is the soldier different from the engineer or the industrialist or the business executive? Modern war calls for the orchestration of a wide range of specialized functions. Men must be trained, supplies and equipment provided for, and all these transported great distances to arrive at particular times. War is a large-scale enterprise, and, like other large-scale enterprises, it has been bureaucratized. The skills of the officer are those of the executive and administrator in any large bureaucracy, of planning and of coordinating the efforts of teams of specialists. If he has the skills of the executive, the officer can also be expected to have his bureaucratic rigidities, and there is no question that the business executive does have bureaucratic rigidities. After all, it has been the businessman and not the soldier who has been dubbed the "organization man."

It is perhaps useful to repeat that it was a soldier, General Ridgway, who in effect vetoed the plan for an American intervention in Vietnam in 1954. It was not the military who decided to make Vietnam an American war in 1965; the military were in general opposed to any limited land war on the mainland of Asia.

Even though the stereotype of the archconservative, rigid militarist has little validity when applied to the American military, and even though the concept of the "military mind" is more confusing than helpful, there is still a danger in the increased role the military play in the making of national policy. It seems reasonable to expect that anyone, civilian or soldier, who is given responsibility for a nation's security would become preoccupied with the power aspects of policy problems. In this sense any secretary of defense, if he does the job he is given to do, would also develop a "military mind" and very quickly. It not only seems inevitable that both military and civilian officials will come to put the power aspects of problems central in their concern, but desirable. So long as it is a world of sovereign nation states, to repeat, we must look to our own security. Our security is the job the military have been given to do, and no one wants to see them neglect it.

Beyond the job of providing for our security, the military must be responsible for still another point. The fact is that for most foreign policy problems today, some sort of military advice is absolutely vital. Although the tension of the cold war has lessened, it is not over. The world contains many other potential dangers. No one knows what direction China will take in the years ahead, for one example; for another, new nationalisms are on the march in Asia, Africa, and the Middle East, whose ultimate directions are equally unclear. It is a world of turmoil and violence. And what gives the task of meeting a potential threat an almost exquisite complexity is that it is posed concurrently with a technological revolution, involving missiles and electronics as well as nuclear warheads, that is so fundamental as to cast the entire structure of strategic doctrine into disarray. As it goes forward and increases in tempo, this revolution in strategy is creating new relationships among all the elements of international politics. It seems obvious that no statesman will be able to develop effective foreign policies without continuous advice from military specialists. A real danger does exist that the military's inevitable concern with power will give national policy an excessive emphasis on force. But it is both sterile and dangerous to try to prevent this by confining the military to technical military problems and isolating them in a kind of military quarantine where they can have no effect on diplomatic and policy problems.

The way to avoid having the military's concern with the power aspects of problems from giving national policy an excessive emphasis on force is, first, to see that the military have an understanding of political and economic matters as well as military ones. In part at least, this need is already being met in the service schools, not only at the undergraduate level in West Point, Annapolis, and the Air Force Academy, but also in the postgraduate command and general staff colleges and the war colleges. The purpose is not to equip the officer to make the political and economic judgments rightly belonging to civilians, but to enable him to understand the context in which his advice on military matters must be judged and so to be more effective in adapting military means to the political necessities laid down by higher authority.

The second and even more important way of ensuring that the power of the military and their preoccupation with the power aspects of policy problems do not give national policy an excessive emphasis on force is to make sure that they do not have the field for themselves. If the military aspects of policy problems are to be considered only in their political context, then it is essential that both the State Department and the White House staff be peopled with strong and able men, preferably men with some political leverage in their own right, who can serve as vigorous spokesmen for those political considerations.

The Central Intelligence Agency

Until World War II the United States paid little attention to intelligence work. In the 1920s, for example, when Henry L. Stimson became Secretary of State, he disbanded the embryonic cryptographic section with the statement that "Gentlemen do not read each other's mail."[3]

[3] Henry L. Stimson and McGeorge Bundy, On Active Service in Peace and War (1947), p. 188.

The only permanent organizations devoted to intelligence were the Navy's Office of Naval Intelligence and the Military Intelligence Division of the General Staff. Although these had the authority to conduct espionage and to maintain estimates of the world situation, they could never get the money to do very much more than supervise the military attachés, maintain an order of battle estimate on the major powers, and perhaps occasionally sponsor an individual secret agent on a temporary job.

With the coming of World War II, the military intelligence organizations were given the means to expand their efforts, but an even more important development was the establishment of the Office of Strategic Services (OSS), under "Wild Bill" Donovan. William J. Donovan had led the Fighting 69th in World War I, winning his nickname and a Congressional Medal of Honor, and after the war he had returned to his law practice and an interest in New York politics. In 1940 and 1941, President Roosevelt enlisted Donovan for two confidential missions to Europe and the Middle East, and on these trips Donovan was shown the details of what the British were doing in espionage, resistance movements, and commando operations. A keen and interested observer, Donovan learned much and apparently put every bit of it into practice when the President asked him to set up the OSS, which was essentially a central intelligence agency. Not that the OSS was restricted to intelligence work only—Donovan's receptivity and enthusiasm made him willing to add a branch of OSS to perform almost any role anyone could suggest. The result was a lighthearted hodgepodge. Among the earliest branches were those concerned with research and analysis, espionage, and "black propaganda" (propaganda purporting to come from enemy sources). In addition there were branches concerned with sabotage and commando-type operations, guerrilla work with the resistance movements, and various odd intelligence jobs such as collecting and analyzing for military purposes the snapshots taken by American tourists in the years before the war.

In the immediate postwar period, a battle royal took place

in Washington over whether or not to retain OSS as a permanent central intelligence agency. Eventually the supporters of OSS won. Title I, Section 102 of the National Security Act of 1947 established the Central Intelligence Agency as an independent organization reporting to the National Security Council. To avoid the spectacle, seen several times during World War II, of secret agents sponsored by one of the military services stumbling over the agents sponsored by another, the CIA was given a legal monopoly of espionage and covert operations of all kinds. The CIA was also given responsibility for coordinating the research and analysis intelligence work done in the various departments —the work of G-2 of the Army, A-2 of the Air Force, the Navy's Office of Naval Intelligence, and the Bureau of Intelligence Research in the Department of State. As a practical matter, this latter responsibility means that the CIA serves as chairman of interdepartmental committees that develop the so-called National Intelligence Estimates.

Organization of the CIA

The director of Central Intelligence wears two hats. He is the coordinator of the intelligence community, which is composed of all the departmental intelligence organizations as well as the CIA itself, and he is chief of the CIA. In his capacity as coordinator, the director chairs the United States Intelligence Board, composed of the heads of each of the departmental units; it is this board that is the instrument of coordination. The CIA itself is composed of a variety of special subunits, ranging from experts in the forging of travel documents to economic research units whose major source of information is the statistical abstracts of the United Nations. Basically, however, the organization is divided into two parts, one concerned with plans and operations under the deputy director for plans, and the other concerned with all aspects of research and analysis, including the preparation of the National Intelligence Estimates, under the deputy director for intelligence.

Criticism of the CIA

In recent years the CIA has come under increasing criticism. One reason for the criticism has been a series of mistakes— even fiascos—that have become public scandals. The most notable was the Bay of Pigs. President Kennedy blamed himself for this disaster, but he also drew a lesson from it—that he "would have to deal with the CIA." Even earlier, in the Eisenhower Administration, there had been a number of similar cases—aid to the 1958 rebellion in Indonesia, during which an American pilot was captured and held prisoner; the allegation that the CIA was deeply involved in maintaining Chinese Nationalist Kuomintang troops on the territory of Burma; and a variety of situations, such as Laos, where the CIA was reported to be pursuing policies that undercut the ambassador.

But the problem is certainly more fundamental than particular mistakes or errors in judgment. President Truman, during whose Administration the CIA had been established, expressed some of this concern in a public statement in 1963. "For some time I have been disturbed," he wrote, "by the way CIA has been diverted from its original assignment. It has become an operational and at times a policy-making arm of the government."[4] Truman went on to say that he never had any thought when he set up the CIA that it would be injected into peace-time cloak-and-dagger operations, but that he intended it to be confined to intelligence work. "Some of the complications and embarrassment that I think we have experienced are in part attributable to the fact that this quiet intelligence arm of the President has been so removed from its intended role that it is being interpreted as a symbol of sinister and mysterious foreign intrigue—and a subject for Cold War enemy propaganda." President Truman's conclusion was that he would like to see the CIA restored to its original assignment as the intelligence arm of the President. "We have

---

[4] In an article syndicated by the North American Newspaper Alliance, as it appears in the *Washington Post*, Dec. 22, 1963.

grown up as a nation," he wrote, "respected for our free institutions and for our ability to maintain a free and open society. There is something about the way the CIA has been functioning that is casting a shadow over our historic position and I feel that we need to correct it."

President Truman's role in creating the CIA makes his criticism all the more sobering. But, stiff though his criticism was, others have been even harsher. Article after article in magazines and newspapers catalogued a long list of charges: that the CIA was a mass of bumbling inefficiency; that it was a citadel of extreme conservatism; that it had vast sums of money at its disposal for which it made no accounting; that it had such an extensive empire and so many employees that in some of our embassies overseas the CIA agents outnumbered regular foreign service officers; that the pervasive secrecy of intelligence activities permitted the CIA to pursue its own policies without regard for the rest of the government; that when an intelligence agency combined policy and operations with intelligence gathering, as the CIA did, there was an inevitable tendency to warp the intelligence it gathered to suit its particular policy preferences; and that the atmosphere of plot and intrigue inevitably spilled over into the domestic arena, threatening the very system the intelligence agency was supposed to protect. Some of these charges were undoubtedly motivated by nothing more than sensationalism. But some of the concern was very real. Two responsible journalists, one the head of the *Herald Tribune's* Washington Bureau, went so far as to write a book which charged that there were "two governments in the United States today," one visible and the other invisible. They were convinced that "the Invisible Government has achieved a quasi-independent status and a power of its own," with the result that one cannot help suspecting "that the foreign policy of the United States often works publicly in one direction and secretly through the Invisible Government in just the opposite direction"—sometimes, the authors seem to suggest, against the wishes of the President himself.[5]

[5] David Wise and Thomas B. Ross, *The Invisible Government* (1964).

The basis for fear of the CIA

The root fear is that the CIA represents a *Staat-im-Staat,* a state within a state, and certainly the basis for fear is there. In its network of agents overseas, the CIA has the means for gathering the necessary information on which policy must be based. In its staff of researchers and in the Board of National Estimates in Washington, which are all under the Deputy Director for Intelligence, it has a "little State Department" of people qualified to analyze that information and reach policy conclusions. Because of its method of operating out of embassies—which all intelligence services do, incidentally—it has representation abroad and contact with high officials of foreign governments through which policy can be implemented. Indeed, because the CIA can keep its men in a particular country longer than most ambassadors stay, CIA station chiefs frequently have been able to make closer friendships with prime ministers and kings and presidents than ambassadors do, and thus to be more influential. In many countries, especially certain developing countries which in the height of the cold war were on the firing line of Communist expansionism, where money is used freely in ways that the State Department budget does not provide for and where intrigue is a way of life, most nationals of the country at one time or another sincerely believed that it was the CIA station chief who really represented the United States and not the ambassador. The CIA has all the facilities of an information and propaganda agency, including powerful radio transmitters. At times in the past it has also had independent communications facilities, as mentioned earlier, by which either information or instructions could be sent without any other part of the American government being aware of it. For the implementation of policy, indeed, the CIA at one time or another has had military training centers that have been used to train guerrillas and on at least one occasion—for the Bay of Pigs operation—a brigade of regular troops equipped with artillery. On one or another occasion in the past, it has had airplanes and the pilots to fly them, naval vessels and the crews to man them. With all this it is not surprising that there should be fear that the CIA might develop into a state within a state.

So far the CIA has not become a state within a state, and most of the more extreme charges are not valid. Although the people in the CIA, in common with all other human beings, have made mistakes, the organization possesses a staff of considerable ability. Far from being a haven of extreme conservatism, the CIA during the Eisenhower Administration was the one place that Senator Joseph McCarthy was unable to touch in his witch hunt and was in fact the only place in the Eisenhower Administration that had room for the young activists who wanted to work with youth and labor movements abroad. Through its intelligence-gathering effort, which has relied on scholarly research as much as on cloak-and-dagger operations, the CIA has played a large part, though not the only part, in making the United States government the best informed in the world. In a patient though sometimes painful educational campaign waged through the tedious procedures by which National Intelligence Estimates are developed, it has succeeded in bringing an objectivity—and an overall point of view rising above the parochial interests of the individual military services—that was previously unknown in the American government's analysis of events abroad.

The power of the CIA

The CIA still represents a serious problem, as President Truman said. The problem is one of power.

"The National Security Act of 1947 . . . has given Intelligence," Allen Dulles once said, "a more influential position in our government than Intelligence enjoys in any other government of the world."[6] And he was right. By the time the Kennedy Administration came into office, Allen Dulles had been Director of the CIA for almost eight years, and the CIA's power was at an all-time high.

The CIA, first of all, had a large staff. For example, whereas

[6] In a speech at Yale University, February 3, 1958.

the State Department, at one time had three persons on its Laos desk, the CIA had six. This meant that the CIA could always afford to be represented at an interdepartmental meeting, that it could spare the manpower to prepare the papers that could and sometimes would dominate the meeting, and that it could explore the byways and muster the information and arguments that gave its men authority at those meetings.

As already mentioned, the people in the CIA were outstandingly able, and this was itself a source of power. The agency had stoutly protected its people from Senator Joseph McCarthy and was one of the few places in the government in the Eisenhower era where new ideas were encouraged and activists permitted to do things, and these facts also helped in attracting still more active and able people. Promotion was fast.

The CIA also had money. The exact amount of its budget is still secret, but various newsmen have estimated the total for all United States intelligence activities at about two billion dollars per year, and it is obvious that the CIA's share of the total would be large, certainly amounting to more than the State Department had to spend per year. The CIA's freedom from normal accounting and auditing procedures gave it a flexibility in the use of its money that also gave it power. Paradoxically, the CIA became involved in many activities that its critics considered to be outside its legitimate purview at the urging of other agencies, such as the State Department, who would normally be responsible for the activity but whose budget did not provide for it. Buying books abroad was one example, and helping the impoverished leader of a government-in-exile come to New York to present his case to the UN General Assembly was another. Unhappily, however, where both activities would be accepted as a matter of course had State Department money been available, they became sinister when CIA money was used.

The CIA's command of information was also a source of power. Quite apart from the issue of whether or not information is bent to support a particular point of view, in Washington the first to have a tidbit of information is the first to interpret its significance and is the first to be on the scene when discussion starts on what the policy implications of the information might be. Where information is an asset, command over information is the power to grant or withhold that asset—to a congressman or the press, for example.

Even the need for secrecy can be power. Quite apart from the phenomenon mentioned earlier that in countries where intrigue is a way of life the mere fact of being the secret intelligence service gives prestige that translates into power, the need to keep certain operations or sources of information secret gives those who "need to know" a further dimension for making judgments or understanding the why of what is happening. Those who knew of the peripheral reconnaissance flights that probed Soviet air defenses during the Eisenhower Administration and of the U-2 flights over the Soviet Union itself, for example, were better able to understand some of the things the Soviets were saying and doing than people who did not know of these activities.

The CIA also derived power from the fact that the function it performed, like that of the FBI, is by its nature politically appealing. The CIA was in the forefront of the Cold War. Its job was to smite our enemies, not to negotiate with them, compromise with them, or make agreements with them. It had the appeal of patriotism. In Congress the CIA's natural allies were also the "inner club," the power center of Congress, the men at the heart of the long-standing coalition of southern Democrats and conservative Republicans, the men of long tenure and conservative outlook. A natural alliance with the congressional power center, a mandate so broad that it is called upon to testify as often before the committees on Armed Services and Science and Technology as before the committee on Foreign Relations, and a command of secret information that can itself enhance the position of the members of the congressional committee that receives it—all these are levers which a politically astute director of the CIA can use to great effect on Capitol Hill.

It is no accident that the two men John F. Kennedy felt it necessary to name first as carry-overs into his new Administration were J. Edgar Hoover and Allen W. Dulles.

Political leverage is power. Information is power. Secrecy is power. Speed in communications is power. Ability is power. And sheer numbers of people is power. The CIA has had all these, and during the years of the Eisenhower Administration it had still another source of power, the fact that the Secretary of State, John Foster Dulles, and the Director of the CIA, Allen W. Dulles, were brothers. Allen Dulles probably never presumed on this relationship, but it inevitably had its effects, if only because people believed it did and behaved accordingly.

Immediately after the Bay of Pigs fiasco, President Kennedy turned to an aide and said, "It's a hell of a way to learn things, but I have learned one thing from this business —that is, that we will have to deal with the CIA." The President explored the possibility of asking Congress to change the National Security Act of 1947, but decided that the opposition within Congress itself was too great. His first step was a letter to all the American ambassadors overseas quite clearly giving them authority over all American activities, including inteligence activities, in the country to which they were accredited. Second the President reestablished the old President's Board of Consultants on Foreign Intelligence Activities under a new name, the President's Foreign Intelligence Advisory Board, and gave it a broader mandate—to reexamine the whole range of activities in the entire intelligence community. And some organizational changes were made in the State Department that had the effect of strengthening the director of the Bureau of Intelligence and Research, who had the responsibility of handling CIA proposals for both intelligence and covert action proposals. Shortly thereafter Allen Dulles was asked to resign.

Throughout the remainder of the Kennedy Administration and during the Johnson Administration, the number and range of CIA activities was cut down and its power considerably reduced. Criticism in both the press and Congress was similarly reduced. Nevertheless, the CIA continues and will continue to exercise considerable power. So long as the world is governed not by a single sovereignty but individual nation states, each of which must look to itself for its ultimate security, nations will have not only armies but intelligence organizations as well. And these organizations will continue to have power in the making of national policy.

FOUR
THE
CONGRESS

ANY discussion of the role of Congress in foreign affairs must begin with an acknowledgment of the load of work carried by most Congressmen, and their busyness. The individual congressman carries a formidable burden. He must, first, handle a multitude of matters for individual constituents. He cannot avoid this, and clearly he should not. The individual citizen's access to his congressman is a useful device by which to balance the necessarily impersonal procedures of bureaucracy. Also it is through their work with constituents that congressmen acquire much of the knowledge of values and preferences that sets limits on their voting behavior even if it does not always guide it. This is particularly true when trying to ascertain how strongly one's constituency feels about an issue, for which most other guides, such as public opinion polls, are of little use. And it takes only a short political experience to learn that a minority who hold a view with great intensity will have more political effect than a diffuse majority who believe the opposite, but not very forcefully.

A second element of the congressman's busyness is the formal calendar. He must attend the floor for voting and do his homework on a variety of bills that run the whole gamut of our national life. Finally he has committee work, with its endless hours of listening and mountains of materials for reading. As a result the congressman jumps from subject to subject with a tempo that approaches frenzy. His day begins early and ends late; his week lasts long. Nothing can be given sustained attention; nothing can be carried through to its completion; most projects are only half done. The congressional scene is, in a word, untidy.

On the other hand, one of the first points that today's observer of Congress might note is how well informed some members of Congress are. Among the more attentive and active members, there seem to be at least a few in each major problem area who are just as knowledgeable as the specialists. Even the less attentive and active member can acquire a formidable knowledge of a subject during ten or fifteen years of service on a committee listening to expert briefings—perhaps even more knowledge, if the truth were known, than some secretary or assistant secretary who has been on the job for only a year or two, as is more usual than not.

In this same connection, the contemporary observer might make a special point of how quickly information and ideas arrive on Capitol Hill in our day. The Congress, like the Presidency or any other locus of power, is a target center at which are aimed the activities of many groups with conflicting opinions, within the structure of government as well as outside it. To further its own ends, each of these groups utilizes every form of information and argument it can lay hands on. Thus each congressman has at his disposal what is in effect a far-flung intelligence network numbering at least in the thousands. It is hardly surprising that an active congressman is one of the first to learn of some new idea, discovery, or technique. As an example, he often learns of the results of university research just about as soon as people in other universities do, and sometimes sooner.

Another characteristic that impresses today's observer is the seriousness with which congressmen take their jobs and their sense of responsibility. Indeed, much of what appears to be irresponsibility to the casual observer probably stems from the kind of conceptual framework by which the individual congressman interprets international events, the "pictures in his head" in Walter Lippmann's phrase. A very high proportion of the Congress, for example, are lawyers—over half, it is said[1]—and it could be argued that in consequence of this there is among congressmen a preoccupation with the legal aspects of international relations, with the wording of treaties and resolutions, with establishing which of the parties to a dispute is legally and morally "right" or "wrong." As with all men, some congressmen tend to personify relations between states and to project to international relations motives and behavior patterns generalized from their experience with individual persons. All of which is merely a roundabout way of saying that congressmen have a wide variety of "pictures in their heads" and that their sense of responsibility is exercised in terms of these widely differing sets of assumptions. Apparent, as opposed to actual, responsibility would thus be increased, as would rationality, by improving congressmen's understanding and the quality of assumptions by which they think about international relations. But this is equally true of all the rest of us, and Congress is nothing if not representative.

An observer of Congress today might also note that Congress has a greater freedom in the field of foreign policy than might ordinarily be supposed. For one thing there seem to be relatively few pressure groups at work on foreign policy, quite unlike the solid array that plead unceasingly for their points of view on domestic matters.[2] The interest of producers' groups seems to be concentrated on protection and with what is certainly notable success. But however important a liberal trade policy may be in the long run—in building, for example, a wider and more stable world system—it is doubtful if any country important in our foreign relations regards our tariffs as a major determinant of their immedi-

---

[1] George B. Galloway, *The Legislative Process in Congress* (1953), p. 373.
[2] On interest groups and their function, see also Chap. 6.

ate foreign policy in the present world situation. Japan is a case in point; it suffers as much from our tariff policies as any and more than most, yet power and political considerations keep it aligned with us on most matters.

Beyond their tariff demands, few producers' groups seem to be much concerned with foreign affairs. Witness, for example, their rather half-hearted attempt to capitalize on the foreign aid program in its postwar beginnings, and the fact that their effect was confined principally to the clause reserving half the shipping business for American firms and the disposal of certain agricultural surpluses. The oil companies, with their interests in Latin America and the Middle East, seem to be the only important exception.

Apart from producers' groups, probably the national minorities are most prominent in the lobbies. The most active of these, and by far the most effective, are Jewish organizations advocating support for Israel. Some Irish organizations support the Irish Catholics in Northern Ireland, but there is really little in the issue that engages United States foreign policy directly. The Eastern European minority groups—Poles, Czechs, and so on—generally support a rather firm anti-Communist position. During most of the postwar period, this has been in line with the general position of the United States government, most congressmen, and most of the general public. In general these groups have opposed policies liberalizing relations with their Communist-controlled homelands, but not so actively as to constitute particularly heavy pressure on most congressmen.

Beyond producers' groups and minority organizations, there are few lobbies in the field of foreign affairs. The one notable exception is the so-called China Lobby, whose official name is the "Committee of One Million." This committee was formed to support Chiang Kai-shek and the Kuomintang government and to oppose the admission of Communist China to the United Nations, diplomatic recognition of Communist China, or any liberalizing policies leading toward improved relations between the United States and Communist China.

The committee was very active for many years. It annually solicited congressional signatures for its stand against the admission of Communist China to the UN, and could be counted upon to attack in the most vehement terms anyone who dared to advocate any change in United States policy toward China. In a sense the China Lobby was not an interest group organized by general citizens to put pressure on Congress, but an interest group organized by one set of congressmen to put pressure both on other congressmen and on officials in the Executive branch, and especially the latter. For the principal leaders of the Committee of One Million were Congressman Walter H. Judd of Minnesota and Senator William F. Knowland of California. Both of these men were ardent supporters of Chiang and the Kuomintang and vehement opponents of the Chinese Communists, and they used the China Lobby to further their own views.

By and large then, Congress seems to be somewhat freer from organized pressure when it comes to decide on an issue of foreign policy than it is on domestic policy. It also seems to be rather free from party control or discipline. The national party dispenses only a very little patronage today, and what it does dispense seems to go more to the workers and contributors of the Presidential campaign than it does toward keeping Congress in line. The congressional party dispenses even less patronage on Capitol Hill. In consequence, one would expect that the most important bait for party regularity that is controlled by the congressional party would be committee assignments and chairmanships.

In assigning committee chairmanships party regularity has never been an important consideration, and it is doubtful if it ever will. If there were national party structures of the kind that would permit the national party effectively to deny to rebels the nomination under the party label, there might be some basis for the congressional party using regularity as one of the criteria for assigning chairmanships. Until that time, however, the seniority rule provides a way of making the decision that is beyond bias or favoritism. Though the rule has been criticized because it does not award the chairmanships to the most capable except by accident, neither does it give affront, and this is a valued quality in party structures so fragile as these.

In making committee assignments, as opposed to choosing chairmen, the party does apparently consider party regularity on occasion. But it is far down the list of criteria, and it seems to be invoked as a general rule only when two members in competition for the same post are nearly equal in other respects. Committee assignments seem to be used only rarely to punish transgressions of party discipline.[3] There are exceptions, however, as in the 69th Congress when two Wisconsin representatives were deprived of their committee chairmanships and others were reduced in rank on their committees for supporting the elder La Follette for the Presidency in 1924. But a more typical as well as a more recent example is that of Adam Clayton Powell. A Democrat from the Harlem district of New York City, he supported Eisenhower in the 1956 election, apparently as a protest against the opposition of southern Democrats to civil rights legislation. The reaction among individual Democrats was sharp and included threats to retaliate by denying Powell his committee assignments. In the end, however, no such action was taken. In any case the violations in all these examples were of discipline in national elections and not on particular bills or items in the party's program. On such matters, it seems clear, party pressure is exercised more subtly than by granting or withdrawing overt benefits. The important pressures seem to be more social and psychological: the good opinion of men one respects, the sense of belonging to the club, the fear of being isolated and alone.[4]

This general freedom of Congress to exercise its own

[3] When a man changes parties completely, of course, he will ordinarily lose his privileges, as Wayne Morse did when he declared himself an independent in 1953, in preparation for switching from the Republican to the Democratic party. See Ralph K. Huitt, "The Morse Committee Assignment Controversy," *American Political Science Review* 41 (June 1957).
[4] See Robert A. Dahl, *Congress and Foreign Policy* (1950), p. 50.

discretion in foreign policy means that the individual congressman is not so reluctant to disagree with the President
and the Executive branch as he might otherwise be. Given his
need for publicity and the obvious fact that in conflict lies
news, the individual congressman is sometimes tempted to
disagree for disagreement's sake or, more accurately, for
publicity's.

CONGRESSIONAL FUNCTIONS IN FOREIGN POLICY MAKING

The functions that Congress plays in the making of foreign
policy are at the same time both very obvious and very
elusive. The obvious function is that of public critic. The floor
of Congress constitutes a platform for speeches on foreign
policy from which individual congressmen can sometimes
capture a headline; the majority and minority leaders and
chairmen of the Foreign Relations and Armed Services committees always can, especially if they are criticizing the administration's foreign policy. And the exercise of Congress's
so-called oversight authority by the use of public hearings,
especially since the rise of television, performs the function
of critic writ very large indeed.

The second function, however, is as elusive as the first is
obvious. What it amounts to is a limit-setting function,
vaguely similar to that performed by a board of trustees in
a university. Theoretically the Congress's power over the purse
and its power to pass on treaties would give it the function
of setting overall policy, much as the board of directors does
in many businesses. Yet neither of these formal powers has
this final result. In the first place, some of the most important aspects of foreign affairs do not require specific and
direct appropriations. Programs, but not necessarily policies,
require appropriations. Most of the State Department's budget
is for "salaries and expenses," and granting or withholding
funds is not directly linked with particular policies. The military budget has a direct effect on foreign policies, but as
already described, the military budget also has a sort of spe-

cial political protection. The only significant foreign policies directly linked with appropriations, in fact, are those concerned with foreign aid. Much the same thing can be said of the power of the Senate to pass on treaties. Relatively little foreign policy is embodied in formal treaties, and recent Presidents have gotten around much of even that by the use of Executive agreements. Most foreign policy is defined by what the President and his representatives *say* publicly and privately, by Executive agreements not requiring the consent of Congress, by the acts of recognizing new governments or not, by attending international conferences or not, by the acts of sending American troops here and there, by establishing or not establishing bases, and so on. Most of these are beyond the *direct* reach of Congress, yet Congress quite clearly does have *indirect* control over at least the upper and lower limits of foreign policy.

THE POWER OF THE INDIVIDUAL CONGRESSMAN

This limit-setting function of Congress becomes somewhat clearer in an examination of the power that Congress wields in foreign affairs. Consider first the power of individual congressmen. Certainly the individual congressman can often dominate the headlines. Throughout the Kennedy Administration, for example, Senator Keating of New York was prominent as an opponent of policy toward Cuba, and Senator Dodd of Connecticut was equally prominent as an opponent of policy toward the Congo. Keating took a hard line, calling for stern measures against Castro and against the Soviets when they put missiles in Cuba. Even when the Soviets backed down, he refused to believe that they had actually withdrawn their missiles from Cuba and continued to beat the drums for "action." In the Congo crisis, United States policy was to support the UN effort to prevent the secession of the rich mining province of Katanga, which would have left the rest of the Congo economically helpless. This was opposed by several conservative European powers, who seemed to be most influenced by pressure from business and investment groups who had large interests in Katanga. Senator Dodd took the side of Katanga and became a persistent critic not only of U.S. policy, but of the UN and its conduct of the operation.

The benefit to these particular Senators of picking up a foreign policy issue in just the way they did is obvious. Senator Keating had been a member of the House for many years representing an upstate district. As Senator he needed to become known in New York City and to build a "statesman" image to overcome his rather parochial, conservative record as an upstate Congressman. Senator Dodd had the problem of representing a state that borders New York City and houses commuters who listen to its radio and television and read its newspapers. How does a Senator from either Connecticut or New York get on New York City's radio and TV and on the front page of the *New York Times?* Picking up a continuing foreign policy issue and being the focal point for opposition to State Department policy is not only an effective way, but it is politically cheap. Both Cuba and the Congo offered an opportunity for Senators to take a strong anti-Communist stand, which is always popular, without risk of alienating anyone except the State Department—which hardly counts for much among the voters of New York and Connecticut.

In the Nixon Administration, Senator Goodell adopted the same tactic, but in connection with Vietnam. Goodell, a relatively unknown Republican, had been appointed by Governor Rockefeller to fill the unexpired term of Robert Kennedy, and he had the same problem of exposure to voters who read the *Times* and look mainly at nationwide television. What Goodell finally did was to split with President Nixon on his Vietnam policy, calling for immediate withdrawal. A public stand on Vietnam by a senator undoubtedly influences a number of the public and may be instrumental in swinging one or two other congressmen into opposition, and this has some influence on policy. But a Republican senator would have access to a Republican President, and one can certainly presume that Goodell could have had just as much influence, and perhaps more, by keeping quiet in public while pressing hard in private. It seems clear, in other words, that although Goodell was undoubtedly sincere in opposing the war, opposing it publicly served not to increase Goodell's influence on the Nixon Administration, but only to enhance his public image in the eye of the voter.

What effect did Keating, Dodd, and Goodell have on the substance of foreign policy? Keating attracted attention to the possibility of the Soviets' putting missiles in Cuba, but the government was already so sensitive to that possibility it was quivering.[5] Actually Keating and Goldwater between them almost caused the agreement with the Soviets about withdrawing their troops to break down, which was certainly not in either their or the nation's interest. Dodd was never able to force the government to adopt his policy for the Congo, that of supporting Tshombe and the secession of Katanga. Yet their activities were always a factor taken account of in the policy discussions, and policy was at times either adjusted to accommodate some element of their view so as to disarm them or presented in such a way as to forestall them. For even though they did not become rallying points for an alternative policy, Keating and Dodd had the potential for doing so, especially if the policy the government was actually pursuing failed dramatically. Goodell probably had even less effect, for there were many other, more powerful figures—Fulbright and McCarthy, for instance—who had long since staked more effective claims to be the rallying points for opposition to the war.

THE POWER OF CONGRESS AS A WHOLE

If the power of individual congressmen is limited, what of the power of the Congress as a whole? Consider some examples. In Vietnam during President Kennedy's Administration, Con-

---

[5] See my To Move a Nation, Part 5, "The Cuban Missile Crisis," passim.

gress played a very small role. There was pressure from the liberals in Congress to dissociate the United States from President Diem, whom they regarded as a dictator. But after the Buddhist crisis of 1963, dissociation became the general direction of official policy quite independently of congressional views. The conservatives of both parties agreed with the "hawk" view that advocated bombing North Vietnam and the United States taking over direction of the struggle from the Vietnamese, but they did not make a great effort to get the policy adopted. The irony is that one of the main reasons this group did not push harder for stepping up the war was that the Pentagon, their main ally in the Executive branch, kept stubbornly insisting that the war was already being won. If the war was going well, then there was no real need to bomb the North and take over responsibility from the Vietnamese.

In President Johnson's Administration, Congress played a much bigger role on the Vietnam question. At first, in spite of public doubts from the liberals, Congress went along with President Johnson's policy, even to the extent of passing the Tonkin Gulf resolution by an overwhelming majority. Increasingly, however, the Congress, and especially the Senate Foreign Relations Committee chaired by Senator J. William Fulbright, moved into more active opposition. Fulbright held hearings that gave publicity to the opposition view, and Senators Morse of Oregon, Gruening of Alaska, Church of Idaho, Kennedy of New York, and McCarthy of Minnesota all took prominent parts. Eventually, their opposition had a profound effect in the election year of 1968, when President Johnson was forced to retire from the Presidential race because opposition to his Vietnam policy and to him personally became so fierce. But they did not succeed in *preventing* President Johnson from escalating the war in the first place by his 1965 decision to bomb North Vietnam and to send American combat forces there in strength. Even their final success in forcing Johnson to withdraw came as something of a surprise to them, for by January 1968, the senators and congressmen who opposed the Vietnam War were frustrated and downhearted, convinced that they had exhausted every possibility of bringing about a change in the President's policy.

In each of these examples, both those in which Congress was successful and those in which it was less successful, there runs a common thread—the role that Congress played was almost never direct or initiative taking. And this seems to be true across the board in foreign policy. It is certainly true of the *continuing* problems of foreign policy. It is very rare that Congress takes the initiative in foreign aid, for example. Usually congressional action is to cut, not add. The one exception that comes to mind is the attempt in the House in late 1969 to add $54.5 million for jet fighters for Nationalist China which, typically, was killed by the Senate. The lack of congressional initiative is equally familiar in other continuing problems—in matters such as the Strategic Arms Limitation Talks and the earlier limited nuclear test ban negotiations. This seems equally true of the crises. Although Keating and Goldwater made troublesome speeches and public pronouncements about Cuba, and Dodd made equally troublesome speeches about the Congo, Congress as such played almost no role in either the Cuban missile crisis or the Congo crisis. Neither did it play a significant role in the Berlin crisis, in the more recent Pueblo crisis, or in any others that come to mind.

OBSTACLES TO CONGRESSIONAL INITIATIVE

In domestic policy Congress can occasionally take the initiative and force a new policy according to its tastes, but rarely so in foreign policy. In foreign policy the Executive calls the tune, and there are reasons. Although he is a focal point for information, as already mentioned, the congressman cannot handle a large volume of it, and it is only on problems in crisis that he normally focuses, especially in foreign affairs. On day-to-day matters and to an important extent even on crisis matters, it is the Executive who controls the detailed flow of information from overseas. There need be no conscious intention to suppress one kind of information and emphasize another to accomplish the same result as deliberate suppression and emphasis. Few people with an intimate knowledge of government believe that United States officials deliberately and consciously lied about how the war was going in Vietnam, for example, but everyone acknowledges that wishful thinking, self-delusion, and defensiveness in fact did lead to the distortion of information. Congressmen did become the focus for information pointed in the opposite direction, but they could not be certain about the reliability of their information and were hesitant to put themselves against the authority of the Executive or reluctant to join those who did.

Even when passions run less deep than they did over Vietnam, the policy position of the Executive will have its effect on the way information is presented. In such a massive flow of information, merely winnowing the raw data down to what one man could conceivably absorb would of itself present a partisan picture of the situation.

The increasing technicality of foreign affairs also robs the Congress of its power. Understanding the Buddhists in Vietnam, the nature of the new nationalism, the complexities of the Sino-Soviet dispute, and so on require expert knowledge, and it is the Executive who has the greater command of experts. As a consequence, it is the Executive who sets the framework in which policies are discussed, who defines the problems we will essay as a government and the alternatives from which we choose the courses of action to meet them.

This command of both information and expertise gives the Executive the intellectual initiative in making foreign policy. The Congress as a whole can criticize; it can add to, amend, or block an action by the Executive. But Congress can succeed only occasionally in forcing Executive attention to the need for a change in policy, and rarely can it successfully develop and secure approval from the public for a policy of its own.

The Executive also has an "instrumental" initiative in foreign affairs. It is the Executive who carries out a policy, who deals with problems face to face. In doing so he must inevitably make a host of secondary decisions that can and do set new lines of policy. Here again, this is especially true in foreign policy. It is the Executive who conducts negotiations with other powers, and in these negotiations it can make promises and commitments that Congress cannot fail to honor. Frequently, indeed, the Executive may proceed without any formal reference to Congress at all. President Kennedy concluded the Laos agreements of 1962 without formal reference to Congress, President Eisenhower's commitment to South Vietnam in 1954 was not formally referred to Congress and neither was Kennedy's in 1961. And there is a host of other examples: Roosevelt's destroyers-for-bases deal with Great Britain; the Yalta agreement, which so many congressmen resented for so long; Truman's decision to meet the blockade of Berlin with an airlift; and his even bolder decision to use American troops in Korea in 1950.

Even the attempts the Congress occasionally makes to get in on what Senator Vandenberg used to call the "take offs" of foreign policy as well as the "crash landings" frequently illustrate only how pitifully weak the Congress is in exercising direct control or in playing an initiative-taking role.

An example of Congress attempting to exercise direct control occurred in late 1969 over the issue of American troops in Laos and Thailand. Badly burned over the experience of Vietnam, where President Johnson had sent over a half a million men with no other congressional authorization than the vague Tonkin Gulf Resolution, which many congressmen felt was deliberately misinterpreted by President Johnson, the Congress was shocked to learn through the hearings conducted by Senator Symington of Missouri that there were American troops stationed in Thailand and that the United States was supporting a "secret army" of Meo tribesmen in Laos sponsored by the CIA. As a result the Congress passed a resolution expressing the sense of the body that the President should not send troops to either Laos or Thailand in the future without a prior congressional resolution. Two aspects of this action, however, are instructive. The first is that enough congressmen were sufficiently uneasy about tying the President's hand in some future crisis to defeat the resolution and would have done so if President Nixon had not let it be known that the resolution was in line with the Administration's policy. The second point is that a resolution does not have the binding effect of law, and if there were a crisis in the future sufficiently grave and sufficiently urgent to permit the President to justify sending American troops to Laos or Thailand on grounds of protecting the national security, there would in fact be no legal barrier. The resolution, in other words, is nothing more than the expression of a pious hope that the President will consult with Congress before making such a decision if it is possible and feasible to do so.

An example of Congress trying to play an initiative-taking role was the attempt to bring about a reduction in the number of American troops stationed in Europe. In 1951 during the Korean War, when tension between the United States and the Soviet Union was at its height, the United States stationed some seven divisions in Europe with NATO. Following the successful ending of the Cuban missile crisis in 1962, however, and the signing of the limited nuclear test ban treaty in 1963, tensions subsided. Many observers saw the beginnings of a detente between the United States and the Soviet Union, and many more, including most Europeans, became convinced that the Soviet Union no longer posed a threat to Europe. Senator Mansfield, as majority leader of the Senate, repeatedly called for a reduction in the number of American troops stationed in Europe, both as an economy measure and as a step that would contribute to the growing detente. Senator Mansfield was successful in enlisting the support of the Senate Foreign Relations Committee, but not in getting the Congress as a whole to express support for a troop withdrawal. Even if he had, however, it would not have been binding on the President. But even though they have not been successful, Senator Mansfield's activities have had the effect

of putting a certain level of pressure on the President to justify the decision to keep the troops there. If the President
does decide at some future date to withdraw the troops,
Senator Mansfield's efforts will have created a political climate
in which the President's decision will require less effort from
the President himself.

THE LIMIT-SETTING POWER OF CONGRESS

This weakness of the Congress in exercising direct control or
in taking initiatives and the power of the Executive to proceed
in so many matters without reference to Congress or even to
evade the expressed desires of Congress is only part of the
story. Congress participates only fitfully in the actual formulation of foreign policy and takes formal action only in approv-
ing or rejecting appropriations, treaties, resolutions, and in
confirming the appointments of ambassadors and high officials. Yet it is equally clear that Congress—subtly and indirectly, but nevertheless effectively—plays a decisive role in
setting the tone of many policies and the limits on many
others.

The most dramatic example of the power of Congress to set
the policy tone is the case of China policy over the twenty-
five years since World War II. Congress and congressmen
took the lead in solidifying a national consensus on a rigid
policy toward Communist China, and the viciousness of the
McCarthy era made it concrete. Once this kind of wide consensus is fixed, inertia rules. It then takes almost heroic action
to overcome even the mildest congressional resistance. President Kennedy wished to bring about a change in China policy,
but progress was painfully slow. In the beginning of his Administration, he sought to start by recognizing Mongolia, but
the Nationalist government on Taiwan objected, and their
friends in Congress quickly shot the proposal down. Nothing
dramatic or specific would have been accomplished by recognizing Mongolia; the effects would have been symbolic and
psychological, foreshadowing a *coming* change in China pol-

icy. This was the trouble, for when the purpose is a change in policy against a massive inertia of the kind surrounding policy toward China, it is essential to have quick results to point to and help beat off counterattacks.

Legally and constitutionally President Kennedy could have gone ahead and recognized Mongolia and followed it with other steps leading to a basic change in China policy. But he would have had to be willing to take the consequences, not just angry speeches and threats of impeachment, but retaliatory action on a whole range of other matters over which Congress has more direct legal and constitutional power. To be specific, if Kennedy had gone ahead and recognized Mongolia at that time, appropriations for both the Alliance for Progress and for Kennedy's aid program for Africa would have been very heavily cut. Kennedy chose to wait for another and better day.

It is here that the peculiar and somewhat elusive power of Congress lies. In one sense the power of Congress in foreign affairs is a negative, limit-setting power—the power of deterrence and the threat of retaliation. On some specific detail of a foreign policy, the President may frequently ignore the Congress with complete impunity, but on the overall, fundamental issues that persist over time, he must have their cooperation and acquiescence, even if he is not required to have their formal and legal consent. Although he may ignore individual congressmen, even powerful committee chairmen, collectively he must bring them along in any fundamental policy. Here again, he is the "President-in-sneakers" trying to induce the congressmen and senators to "climb aboard."

FIVE
THE ROLE OF
THE ELECTORATE

F OR generations political scientists in America clung to an ideal of policy making in democracy in which the electorate was to decide among rival policies as well as choose among rival leaders. The view was most eloquently voiced by Woodrow Wilson, when he was still a professor, in his book, *Congressional Government*. Wilson pined for the logic and clearly fixed responsibilities of parliamentary government modeled on what he conceived to be the British system of his day. He admired the party discipline the British displayed and the clear-cut choices of policy that their system at least *appeared* to offer the electorate. Congress, on the other hand, appalled him. He was convinced that its noisy and often undignified procedures were an insurmountable obstacle to good government. Its untidiness outraged his Calvinist soul.

The truth of the matter is that the British system never did work the way Wilson and his intellectual followers thought it did. If it had, the results would undoubtedly have been disastrous. The few examples where the two parties momentarily approximated the ideal and offered grand policy alternatives which they insisted on following have not been happy ones. The postwar nationalization and denationalization of the steel industry as the Labor and Conservative parties came in and out of office are only suggestive of the wrenches the British economy and society would have been subjected to. Instead of offering grand policy alternatives, the parliamentary system, like the congressional system, works to find compromises that blur the alternatives rather than sharpen them.

But the Wilsonian ideal does not die easily. It was responsible for the referendum movement, which reached something of a peak in California, and it forms the philosophical underpinning of the various recurrent efforts in voter education.

SCHUMPETER AND THE CLASSICAL DEFINITION OF DEMOCRACY

The most vehement of the many attacks on the classical definition of democracy was probably that launched by Joseph A. Schumpeter in his book, *Capitalism, Socialism, and Democracy;* at the same time Schumpeter also offered one of the more persuasive alternative definitions. The key assumption in the classical definition, according to Schumpeter, was the notion of the "common good," which was to be the beacon light of policy. The notion of the "common good" implies that any rational man can see it, that is, that it takes no special knowledge or training to be able to identify the common good. The notion of the common good also implies that it contains the answer to all policy questions; every measure is either good or bad. In the ideal democracy, then, it is both plausible and feasible for the people to decide on issues, for the people to determine policy. In a very large community, however, the affairs of government take up so much time that some compromise with this ideal becomes necessary. The people therefore should decide only the most important of the issues, by referendum or as an integral part of elections (i.e., by choosing between parties offering alternative policies), and through elections appoint a committee (a representative legislature) to determine policy on lesser issues. In the case of parliamentary democracies, this committee in turn appoints a smaller committee (the Cabinet or Executive) and a chairman (Prime Minister) to execute the policies determined. In the case of a congressional democracy, the chairman is separately elected and appoints his executive committee with the advice and consent of the policy-determining committee.

The question that Schumpeter poses, with considerable scorn, is, whose is the common good? It is precisely the struggle of politics to determine whose good shall be the common good. The common good furthermore not only means different things to different people, but it means different things to the same people.

Not even compromise necessarily reflects the majority will. "The chances for this to happen," Schumpeter writes, "are greatest with those issues which are quantitative in nature or admit of gradation, such as the question how much is to be spent on unemployment relief provided everybody favors some expenditure for that purpose."[1] But in the case of qualitative issues, such as whether to persecute heretics or to enter upon a war, a compromise may be equally distasteful to everyone. Schumpter argues in fact that in such circumstances a decision imposed by a nondemocratic agency will often prove more acceptable than a compromise. He gives as an example Napoleon's action on the church issue when he was First Consul and the head of a military dictatorship. Napoleon imposed a settlement that gave a certain amount of religious freedom while strongly upholding the authority of the state. Any "democratic" attempt at solution, Schumpeter argues, would have been a disaster: "Deadlock or interminable struggle, engendering increasing friction, would have been the most probable outcome of any attempt to settle the question democratically. But Napoleon was able to settle it reasonably, precisely because all those groups which could not yield their points of their own accord were at the same time able and willing to accept the arrangement if imposed."

Having rejected the classical theory of democracy with its

[1] Joseph A. Schumpeter, *Capitalism, Socialism, and Democracy* 2nd ed., p. 255.

assumption of a common will and goal of having the people actually decide on particular issues, Schumpeter offers an alternative definition. Democracy, according to his definition, is government in which there is competition for political leadership, and the role of the people is not to decide on issues but to produce a government. Democracy, he writes, "is that institutional arrangement for arriving at political decisions in which individuals acquire the power to decide by means of a competitive struggle for the people's vote."

Schumpeter argues that his definition has a number of advantages over the classical definition. First, it provides a practical test, one that can be used in the real world. Second, it leaves room for the role of leadership, noticeably lacking in the classical theory. Third, insofar as a group-wide "good" or "will" exists—say, minority groups, or labor, or the unemployed—Schumpeter's theory leaves ample room for the group to act in terms of their collective good, that is, a minority group can vote for leadership on the basis of the leadership's policy stand on the issue affecting the particular group. Thus the theory provides for competition, but as in economic life the competition is not perfect.

Schumpeter's theory, too, explains the indirect control of the electorate. The role of the people is primarily to make a government, and this implies the function of evicting it. So the electorate does not control policy decisions while the government is in power, but only evicts it on stated occasions and circumstances if it is displeased with the results that the government achieves. Hence the influence of the electorate on policy during the term of the government is the threat of throwing the government out if it does badly, leaving the government to find out, if it can, not so much whether the electorate approves of given policies, but the further step of whether or not the final *results* of given policies will or will not please the electorate. It does not really matter, for example, if the majority of the people at the time thought that bombing North Vietnam in 1965 was a good policy. The important thing is that the majority of the people came to be dissatisfied with the result, the fact that the bombing did not bring the war to a successful conclusion, that women and children were killed, and that the results of the action were evil.

Schumpeter, finally, argues that his theory also explains more satisfactorily than the classic theory some of the consequences of democratic society, especially the relationship between democracy and individual freedom. He points out that no society tolerates absolute freedom and no society reduces freedom to zero. Democracy, he argues, does not necessarily grant more individual freedom than other political systems; it may, in fact, be the other way around. The relation between democracy and freedom is that if in principle at least everyone is free to compete for political leadership, then in most cases this will mean a considerable freedom of discussion for all and will normally mean a considerable amount of freedom for the press.

DEMOCRATIC THEORY AND VOTER BEHAVIOR

It can be admitted that the classical theory of democracy is unreal in its assumptions about the common good and impractical in its striving for a situation in which the electorate decides on policy issues. It can also be admitted that even if it is accepted, Schumpeter's theory still leaves ample room for the electorate to *influence* policy choices. In the first place, as Schumpeter himself says, if one or another group does in fact perceive a common good or will for that group on a particular policy issue, it can vote for leadership that promises that kind of policy. Certainly blacks in recent times when civil rights has been a central issue, have voted as a bloc for leadership that favored civil rights. If a minority group can vote its policy preferences in choosing leadership, so can everyone else. This still leaves a further influence—that the incumbent government shapes its policies with some knowledge of probable voter reaction and in anticipation of that reaction. Thus the issue becomes to what extent voters vote for one set of leaders over another because the one set represents policy positions closer to the voter's own policy preferences.

Much of the research on voter behavior is not encouraging for supporters of democratic theory. In the 1948 election, for example, it seems that some people voted for Truman and against Dewey because they disliked Dewey's mustache. In the 1960 election, a number of "little old ladies" apparently voted for Kennedy because he and Jackie made such a charming couple. Nixon, on the other hand, lost votes because of his "five o'clock shadow" on television and his "shifty eyes."

Admittedly, people who voted for such obviously irrational reasons are only a very, very tiny minority. But many of both the practitioners and observers of politics have assumptions about the intelligence and sense of responsibility of the mass of the voters that are on just about the same low level. A great deal of attention, for example, is paid by the practitioners of politics to television techniques, and one recent book in effect ascribes Richard M. Nixon's election in 1968 to a slick television presentation in which the candidate's "image" was supposedly made over and sold to a gullible public as if it were soap.[2]

But even on a more sophisticated, scientific, and objective level, the findings of research on voter behavior have not been very encouraging. Personality, for example, seems to play a large role. One thinks of Roosevelt's storied charm, for example, and Eisenhower's warm friendliness. And there is the undisputed fact that an incumbent President has an advantage, apparently derived at least partly from the mere fact that people *think* of him as the President.

Then, there is the apparent decisiveness of past party association. Of all the determinants of voter behavior, the fact of which party one's parents voted for seems to be the single most important. Most people who vote Republican apparently had parents who voted Republican; most people who vote Democratic had parents who voted Democratic.

[2] J. McGinniss, *The Selling of the President, 1968* (1969).

Even though most people stick blindly to their party and the party of their fathers, democratic theory might still be salvaged if the so-called independent voters exercised their intelligence and reason, for it is those who switch from party to party that presumably determine who will win the election. What is particularly discouraging is that the research findings about people who describe themselves as "independents" indicates that they are among the least well informed, among the least involved politically, and among the most impressionable and even frivolous in their voting decisions.[3]

Still other voter studies seem to indicate that people vote according to social determinants—economic status, religion, education, urban, rural, or suburban residence, and membership in minority or ethnic groups—which implies that the individual voters behave as blindly and unintelligently as sheep.

AN ALTERNATIVE THEORY: V. O. KEY

These findings, however, were persuasively challenged by the late V. O. Key in what was to be his last book, *The Responsible Electorate*. What Key did was to examine the Roosevelt-Truman elections of 1932, 1936, 1940, 1944, and 1948; the Eisenhower elections of 1952 and 1956; and the Kennedy election of 1960 to determine which policy issues came to the fore. He then divided the voters into (1) standpatters, that is, those who voted in any one of these elections for the same party that he voted for in the election four years earlier; (2) switchers, that is, those who changed parties; and (3) new voters, that is, those who came of voting age in the interim or who for one reason or another did not vote in the previous election. He then tried to determine whether there were significant correlations between the policy preferences of the three different types of voters on the issues of the particular campaign and the way they finally voted.

[3] Cambell et al., *The American Voter*, pp. 143–145.

Key's first finding is that the previous assumption that few voters switch from their traditional party is quite wrong. We are accustomed to looking at *net change,* which is misleading. In 1952, for example, Eisenhower polled 55.4 percent of the major-party vote and 57.8 percent in 1956. "Then," Key writes, "one may slip easily into the belief that from 1952 to 1956 only 2.4 percent of the 1952 voters changed their allegiance; in fact, five or six times as large a proportion switched their preference. The figure of 2.4 is a measure of *net change* resulting from shifts from Democratic to Republican and from Republican to Democratic and the addition of new voters to each side (as well as the subtraction of former voters from each side); it is a figure that conceals more than it reveals."[4] From one eighth to one fifth of the voters shifted their vote from one party to another in the elections Key studied, and new voters made up between 15 to 20 percent of the voters in each of these elections. Thus the impression that the electorate remains fairly static is false. "Instead a vast and intricate churning about occurs as millions of voters switch party preferences. Millions more enter the active electorate; they have become of age or have decided to vote this time after not having voted for one reason or another at the previous election." A relatively small number of the switchers are the independents on which previous studies focused.

In one particular election, then, as many as one fifth of the voters switch, as many as another one fifth are new voters, and three fifths are standpatters. On the face of it, the fact that such a high percentage are making or having to make decisions is encouraging for supporters of democratic theory, depending, of course, on *why* people decide to shift, to stand pat, or, if they are new voters, to go to this party or that one.

The "responsible electorate"

Key concludes on the basis of his research that most voters vote because of their policy preferences, and that they do so

[4] V. O. Key, *The Responsible Electorate,* pp. 16–17.

about as rationally and intelligently as could be expected, given the information available to them and the frequent ambiguity and confusion of the policies put forward in campaign debate. "The perverse and unorthodox argument of this little book," he writes, "is that voters are not fools. To be sure, many individual voters act in odd ways indeed; yet in the large the electorate behaves about as rationally and responsibly as we should expect, given the clarity of the alternatives presented to it and the character of the information available to it." His research findings are that the voter is not "strait-jacketed by social determinants or moved by subconscious urges triggered by devilishly skillful propagandists." On the contrary, his findings are that the electorate is "moved by concern about central and relevant questions of public policy, of governmental performance, and of executive personality."

Key's evidence indicates that in several elections of the Roosevelt-Truman era, the overriding issue was the rather general one of the American-style welfare state symbolized by the "New Deal." But the policy issues could also be very very specific. In 1936, for example, the old-age annuity provisions of the Social Security Act were a major issue. Something like 4 out of every 10 Democrats who opposed this particular piece of legislation shifted to vote Republican, and about 3 out of every 10 Republicans who favored the plan shifted to Roosevelt. Other issues that have moved voters according to Key's evidence are the question of government regulation of business (1936), farm policy (1940), the Wagner Labor Relations Act (1940), the third term question in the Roosevelt years (1940) and the Taft-Hartley Act which was restrictive on labor (1948). In 1952 when Eisenhower became President, the issues that most influenced voters were labor and industrial unrest, the Korean War, "Communist subversion" against which Senator Joseph McCarthy tilted, and "corruption in government" symbolized by the mink coat that a Truman aide accepted as a gift. In 1960 the issues that seemed to influence voter behavior were the rise of communism to power in Cuba and the so-called missile gap in foreign affairs. In domestic affairs, the issues were unemployment, which had risen greatly toward the end of the Eisenhower Administration, and most importantly, the issue of religion, since Kennedy would be the first Catholic President if elected.

Key's overall conclusions are fundamental to the supporters of democratic theory. He believes his evidence shows first, that switchers switch mainly on policy questions and that new voters, although influenced by parental affiliations, are just as deeply influenced by their personal policy preferences. Even the standpatters, his evidence shows, stand pat mainly because they are satisfied with the performance of their party and with its policy stand in terms of their own policy preferences.

Key finds that the question of personality is important, presumably in terms of the voters' estimation of how particular personalities will perform, but that personality is not dominating. On the question of whether it was Roosevelt's personality and nothing more that gave him his electoral victories, Key says, "It becomes ridiculous immediately if one contemplates what the fate of Franklin Delano Roosevelt would have been had he from 1933 to 1936 stood for those policies which were urged on the country by the reactionaries of the day."

Social determinants

On the question of social determinants—whether people vote according to economic status, religion, education, urban, suburban, or rural residence, and membership in minority and ethnic groups—Key rejects the idea that any of these factors *determine* a person's vote. The only time such gross characteristics serve as an accurate indication of how people vote is when (1) there is a policy issue that clearly affects the particular group and (2) the rhetoric of the campaign identifies one party with one side of the issue and the other party with the other side.

The fact that a person is, say, a Negro serves as an index to what he believes and to why he votes as he does only when an election concerns Negroes as Negroes and when the members of the group are aware of the issue and see it as basic among their concerns of the moment. Not every election generates group-related issues which drive a wedge through the electorate along lines easily identified by gross characteristics of the electorate.[5]

"Throwing the rascals out"

One final point that is of particular significance for democratic theory is that Key's findings confirm earlier work indicating that the voters are vengeful, that if they do not like the performance of a party in the past, they vote it out even when the actual candidate is new. In 1952, for example, Adlai Stevenson tried his very best to dissociate himself from the Truman Administration. "Yet voters—or a significant number of them—voted against Mr. Stevenson because they disapproved of Mr. Truman, despite Mr. Stevenson's most adroit efforts in evasion and avoidance." Key also adds

Had Mr. Stevenson not been saddled with responsibility for past Democratic performance . . . the electorate would be deprived of its most effective instrument for control of governments. Happily, too, this institutional custom probably permits the electorate to be utilized to best advantage in the process of popular government. The odds are that the electorate as a whole is better able to make a retrospective appraisal of the work of governments than it is to make estimates of the future performance of nonincumbent candidates. Yet by virtue of the combination of the electorate's retrospective judgment and the custom of party accountability, the electorate can exert a prospective influence if not control. Governments must worry, not about the meaning of past elections, but about their fate at future elections.[6]

POLICY ROLE OF THE MASS PUBLICS

In the light of these findings, what can be said about the influence of the mass public on policy making? The most

[5] *Ibid.,* p. 70.
[6] *Ibid.,* pp. 76–77.

obvious is that *if* a particular issue is debated in an election campaign and *if* the two parties offer different policies for dealing with the issue, the electorate will vote with the party whose policy they prefer and thus the electorate will have determined the policy.[7] Undoubtedly it does on occasion happen that the electorate chooses policies in this way. It would be especially likely on those historical occasions when a whole program of policies is advocated by one party and rejected by another, the outstanding example, of course, being Roosevelt's New Deal program of social welfare measures which was so vehemently opposed by the Republicans.

Admittedly such bold departures as the New Deal are historically rare. The New Deal was really a fundamental change in the role of the state in society or, perhaps, a fundamental change in the organization of society itself. On such questions it is more usual for the two major political parties to differ very little if at all. The complaint of contemporary radicals, indeed, is that the two parties are alike as Twiddly-Dee-Dum and Twiddly-Dee-Dee. The truth is that this is exactly the result one would expect if the view of the majority is to prevail on any issue in which the majority is a very large majority and in which the majority view is well known or easily determined. If a graph of mass opinion takes the form of a bell curve and the view of the mass is to prevail, then both parties will take positions only very slightly to the right or left of the absolute center. And the policy preferences of the mass of the people is in fact being followed.

In most elections the issues are not the fundamental organization of society but a mixture of unrelated, individual items, and no one can really tell whether the majority who voted for the winning candidate did so *because* of his policy stand on one particular issue or *in spite of* his policy stand on that particular issue. In the 1948 election, for example, the Taft-Hartley Act, which was restrictive on labor unions, was one of the issues. Key's evidence is that for a number of voters their

[7] In similar fashion the electorate rewards good past performance and punishes bad.

policy preference on this issue caused them to switch to or away from Truman or, in the case of new voters, caused them to become Republicans or Democrats. Because he won the election, Truman claimed he had a mandate to change this law. Now he could not claim that mandate on the grounds that a *majority* favored a change in the law, but what he could claim was that he had a mandate to change it because the majority had had an opportunity to reject him if it so opposed his stand on that particular law. The law was an issue in the campaign; he had promised to change it if elected, and he was therefore honor-bound to carry out his promise. He could argue that the majority wanted him to be President knowing that he would change the Taft-Hartley law, and that the majority was made up of people who either wanted to see the law changed or did not care if it was changed in comparison to the other benefits they saw in Truman being President. The point remains that if Presidents consider themselves in some way bound to carry out the policy they advocate in a campaign, the electorate is in fact influencing policy even though the majority view on a particular policy remains unknown or obscured.

This leads to another way in which the mass electorate influences policy. Because they assume that people's votes are influenced by their policy preferences, and because they fully understand that voters take revenge for the results of past policies (whether or not they approved of the policy at the time) as well as past performance, Presidents continually make judgments about the policy preferences of the electorate and shape policy in accordance with those judgments. President Kennedy, for example, in the campaign of 1960 made considerable political hay out of the fact that a Communist, Fidel Castro, had come to power in Cuba during the Eisenhower Administration. But he also was convinced that although the electorate did not like that development, they were not willing to use American troops to remove Castro, and in the campaign Kennedy promised that he would not permit American troops to be used for that purpose. In the

Bay of Pigs fiasco, he stuck to that position in spite of considerable pressure from within the government, and the public reaction convinced him even more that the electorate did not want American troops used in that way, *either in Cuba or elsewhere.* In the Laos crisis of 1962 and on several occasions in the continuing crises in Vietnam, he used to say, "If the American people don't want me to use troops to remove a Communist government ninety miles off our coast, how can I ask them to send troops nine thousand miles away?" The point is that even though it was not asked specifically and formally to express itself on this particular issue, the electorate did influence the policy chosen. Kennedy looked for evidence on feelings among the mass public on this issue. Whether or not the evidence was full, conclusive, or completely accurate is all open to question. But there was evidence, and Kennedy made a judgment—or at least a prediction—on what the policy preference of the electorate would be on the issue and acted in accordance with that judgment.

All Presidents on all issues make some effort to seek out evidence on the policy preferences of the mass public. They all make some sort of judgment or prediction about what the reaction of the mass public will be, if only to conclude that the public will be apathetic or that it can be manipulated to support the President's policy if the policy becomes an issue in future elections. And one way or the other all Presidents take the possible reaction of the mass public into account in shaping their policies.

SIX
PUBLIC OPINION,
INTEREST GROUPS, AND THE PRESS

THE conclusion of the preceding chapter stressed that all Presidents take into account the possible reaction of the mass public in shaping their policies. If this conclusion is correct, then the question of the influence of the individual members of the mass electorate on policy becomes one of how the views of the individual voters are expressed and of where and how the President gets evidence on policy preferences in the mass electorate. We are led to look first at the functioning of public opinion; second, at the role of interest groups and organizations; and third, at the role of the press and the media of mass communication, television especially, and radio.

PUBLIC OPINION

One of the first findings of systematic research on public opinion was that there is not just one public, but many. One such study was made in Cincinnati in 1947.[1] A poll showed that 30 percent of the population of Cincinnati were not familiar with the United Nations and its function and that they were similarly

[1] National Opinion Research Center, *Cincinnati Looks at the United Nations,* 1948.

uninformed about other basic facts of foreign affairs. With the cooperation of local civic organizations, newspapers, and radio stations, a campaign was launched to spread information on all these matters—in effect to blanket Cincinnati with information containing the answers to the questions on the poll. After three months of this campaign, the poll was repeated. The results were unchanged—30 percent of the population of Cincinnatti remained as ignorant of the United Nations and other basic facts of foreign affairs as they were before. The people who had gone to the lectures sponsored by the civic organizations, read the articles, and listened to the radio were those who were already interested and informed. Those who were uninterested and uninformed remained so.

The Cincinnati study and others indicated that there was a division of labor among the mass public. Most people had quite clearly reached the practical and sensible conclusion that modern life was too complex for them to be equally well informed on every issue, and they attempted to keep up with only what particularly interested them or with what affected their own lives most closely. Thus one group of people tends to follow foreign policy, while another is more interested in agricultural policy or educational policy. A particular individual, of course, can be a member of more than one "attentive public," but in general there is clearly a tendency to specialize. Thus one can speak of "public opinion" only in a very general sense on very broad issues. In terms of detailed discussions on particular policy issues, "public opinion" is the opinion of a group of people who are sufficiently interested to acquire the information needed to understand the different policy alternatives under debate and to make judgments about them.

Stimulated by the Cincinnati study and others, Gabriel A. Almond, in his *The American People and Foreign Policy*, described the workings of public opinion in terms of "policy and opinion elites" and the "attentive publics" who form their audiences. The policy and opinion elites include the legal and official policy leadership, the President, the secretary of state, and other officials in the Executive branch, the majority leader in the Senate, and various committee chairmen in Congress, including the "official" opposition, that is, the congressional leaders of the opposition party. It also includes nonofficial specialists in the subject matter who speak, write, and are active in other ways—authors, professors, journalists, and opinion leaders of all types. The attentive publics are the audiences for the debates and discussions of the policy and opinion elites—they are the interested and informed public for the particular subject matter.

It is presumably the members of the attentive publics who are the switchers in elections and who ascribe the reason for their switching to their policy preference on a particular policy issue. It is activity among these particular policy and opinion leaders and attentive publics that generates the evidence on policy preferences that Presidents seek out or that comes to them in one way or another. It is such activity that congressmen become aware of and that presumably encourages or discourages them from taking a public stand for or against a particular policy. To the extent that Presidents shape their policies in accordance with what they conceive of as public opinion and congressmen shape their voting and their public stands according to their understanding of public opinion, it is this activity among particular policy and opinion leaders and attentive publics that is responsible.

The implication of all this is that even though the majority does not necessarily declare itself on policy issues, democracy can still be served, at least in the sense that the mass publics can still have an influence on policy as mass publics. The first condition in order for a mass public to be heard is that the press and others must be relatively free to seek out and publish information. Second, there must be no substantial barrier to prevent anyone who has the talent, interest, and motivation from speaking or writing or otherwise taking a public stand on policy issues—that is, from becoming a member of the policy and opinion leadership by his own efforts. Third, individual members of the mass public must be substantially free to read, attend lectures and meetings, and listen to radio and television—that is, free to become members of the attentive public.

These three conditions can be met rather easily; the final condition is more difficult. For if the policy preferences of even the attentive publics and policy and opinion leaders are to have influence, then the official leadership—the President, the secretary of state, congressmen, and so on—must be willing to shape their policies accordingly, because there is no device by which the attentive publics can actually take part in the policy deliberations within the Executive branch itself.

We have already mentioned the one most important incentive for a President and others among the official leadership to take into account the policy preferences of the attentive publics—the fear of retaliation at the next election. This means that the larger the attentive public on a particular issue is, the noisier it is, and the more united it is on what it believes must be done, the more likely it is that the President and the others will listen. From 1949 until at least 1963, for example, the attentive public and opinion leadership on the question of Communist China was so large, so articulate, and so influential that they virtually exercised a veto over any change from the rigid policy of isolating China from the Western world. Another example was the alliance that eventually developed in opposition to the Vietnam War— attentive public, nonofficial policy leadership, and some of the official policy leadership, including people within the Administration as well as Senators such as J. William Fulbright, Robert F. Kennedy, and Eugene McCarthy. By March of 1968, when President Johnson halted the bombings of North Vietnam above the 20th parallel and withdrew his name from the Presidential race of 1968, this particular public was so large and so noisy that the President felt that only a very dramatic act, such as withdrawing from the race, would permit him to continue to administer the country and foreign policy effectively.

At the very least, the existence of a mass public of sufficient size, vociferousness, and consensus on a particular issue would force the President to attempt to outmaneuver it politically, to nullify it, or to build a rival mass public that supported him on the issue. President Kennedy during the Laos crisis of 1962, for example, and to some extent during the Vietnam Buddhist crisis of 1963, found himself opposed by "hawks" within the Administration, by a Congress that wanted the United States to adopt harder line policies toward the Communists, and by an equally hard-line attentive public whose opinion leaders were men like Senator Barry Goldwater in the Congress and by hard-line journalists such as Joseph Alsop and Marguerite Higgins. As a consequence President Kennedy felt it necessary to play the role of opinion leader himself in an attempt to energize a rival attentive public among academics, students, liberals, and intellectuals who would support his efforts at negotiating the neutralization of Laos and in opposing President Diem's authoritarian policies toward the Buddhists in Vietnam. For President Johnson the situation was reversed. He pursued a hard-line policy in Vietnam, culminating in the decision to escalate the struggle in 1965 by bombing North Vietnam and dispatching American combat forces to the South. Increasingly, President Johnson found himself opposed by a mass public of students, academics, and others and in response he attempted to energize the more hawkish opinion leaders and the mass public to which they appealed. In both cases even though the particular President resisted following the demands of the particular public who opposed him, he was forced to react to their views and to spend time and energy developing an opposing, rival public. President Nixon's appeal to the "silent majority" is the same thing, an attempt to build a rival public that supports him to counterbalance an attentive public that does not.

Although it would be extraordinarily difficult to determine in any precise way the amount of influence the various attentive publics actually exercise on policy, the impression is that it is quite substantial, even though subtle and indirect. An examination of Presidential policies and public statements over the past twenty years certainly demonstrates that all the Presidents of the postwar period spent an extraordinary amount of time and energy attempting to build public support for their policies and to counter opposing views. A purist might argue that this is hardly democracy. As we have said, the motive behind this effort is undoubtedly fear of retaliation at election time, and the mass exercises influence not directly but indirectly. What the President or other officials *think* public policy preferences are is what is influential, or even more accurately, what influences policy is the President's *estimate* of the results of the policies and how well these results will fulfill what he *thinks* are the policy preferences of the mass. Also the process is two-way, that is, the President and other officials influence and if they can, change policy preferences of the attentive publics as well as adapt their own policies to those preferences they cannot change. But the fact still remains that even though their influence is direct and even though they are influenced as well as influence, the attentive publics do affect policy.

One might speculate that it is this complex interplay in which the Executive and the attentive publics influence each other that accounts for President Nixon's Vietnamization policy. From his past statements and political history, an outside observer would assume that President Nixon would prefer a victory in Vietnam and that he would resist making any sort of a "deal" with the Communist side by, say, negotiations that led to a coalition government. On the other hand, the opposition to the Vietnam War was so great by the beginning of his Administration that a decision by Nixon to continue President Johnson's policies would have been politically disastrous. So Nixon tailored his policy to maximize his personal policy preferences and minimize the strength of the opposition—the result is Vietnamization, withdrawing American troops while building up the number, quality, and equipment of the Vietnamese troops, rather than a negotiated settlement. The attentive public opposing the war did not get what it wanted by far, but it did influence policy in the direction it wanted. President Nixon, in turn, did not succeed in persuading everyone in his direction, but he did persuade enough to reduce the power of the opposition quite significantly, at least for a time.

INTEREST GROUPS

If fear of retaliation at the next election causes Presidents and congressmen on their own initiative to seek out and at least take into account the policy preferences of attentive segments of the public, there is still another channel through which their views have influence—the activities of interest groups, private associations, and a great variety of other organizations. The mechanism by which their influence is exercised is substantially different from the elected official's fear of retaliation at the polls.

A great deal of research has been done on these organizations and how they influence policy. What emerges is more than just interest groups and lobbies, but what David B. Truman calls an "intermediate structure" of government.

This structure—which in simplest terms includes at least the great array of interest or pressure groups, corporations, trade unions, churches, and professional societies, the major media of communication, the political parties, and, in a sense, the principal state and local governments—this pluralistic structure is a central fact of the distribution of power in the society. It is a structure that is intervening between government at the national level and the rank and file of the population, intervening rather than subordinate or dominating.[2]

How do these many organizations affect policy? The first way has already been mentioned—that although the membership of these organizations may coincide with the attentive publics just discussed, and that as a consequence there is an obvious connection between the way this intermediate structure affects policy and the fear of retaliation at the polls, this

---

[2] This particular quote is from one of Truman's articles, "The American System in Crisis," *Political Science Quarterly* 74 (December 1959), but the full analysis is contained in his book, *The Governmental Process.*

is not the only mechanism by which interest groups and similar organizations affect policy. As V. O. Key says, when the leader of a special interest group threatens that he will tell his membership to punish an elected official at the polls, the gun he points is not really loaded.[3] It is a fact that the leaders of interest groups can deliver the vote of their membership only in very special and dramatic circumstances, basically when the very existence of the organization and the values for which it stands are threatened. Union leadership, for example, can almost never deliver the union vote just because a particular legislator has voted for something the union leadership opposed or against something it favored. The union leadership can usually deliver the vote only when the issue threatens the very existence of unionism or directly threatens the actual jobs of the membership.

The reasons that the leadership of interest groups, trade and professional associations, and so on cannot deliver the vote of their membership are complicated. The most important of these, and the only one that need concern us here, is that people have more than one interest and not only belong to more than one interest group, but make their decisions about voting for a much wider variety of reasons than those associated with a particular interest group. The member of a union may be simultaneously a liberal or a conservative; a Catholic, Jew, or Protestant; a Pole, Spanish American, or Black; he may be interested in foreign affairs or not; and so on and on and on. Being the member of a union may be only one of many variables that affects how he votes. It is only when a central issue of an election campaign, to repeat, strikes directly at the values around which the interest group is organized that the group can mobilize votes.

Functions of interest groups

What, then, is the function that interest groups serve? The major function, many political science observers have con-

[3] V. O. Key, *Public Opinion and American Democracy*, p. 522.

cluded, is the "articulation of interests."[4] It is this function in its widest sense that David B. Truman had in mind in describing the whole array of interest groups and similar organizations as the "intermediate structure" of government. These groups help people define their interests, work out the implications of various proposals, laws, and so on for the interests identified, and frequently help people distinguish between what is only an apparent advantage and their longer-term, enlightened self-interest. Interest groups articulate interests, identify their interests to people, and at the same time identify people sharing an interest to each other and to those holding official responsibility who can do something about satisfying the interest. The function of articulating interests also implies movement in the opposite direction, that is, the transmission downward to the membership of information, interpretation, and potential conflict with other values and interests and with other rival or opposition interest groups.

The function, certainly, is fundamentally necessary, and all large societies have some device to perform it. In both Hitler's Germany and Stalin's Russia, for example, there were various mass organizations performing this "transmission belt" function both upward and downward, even though in both cases membership was mandatory and the instrument was often more a tool of government for its purposes than a tool of the membership for its purposes. Interestingly enough, research on non-Western societies reveals the same function being performed through quite different instrumentalities. Instead of labor unions and granges articulating the interests of working men and farmers, for example, in certain Asian countries the function is performed by the extended family system and and in at least one country—Vietnam—at a certain period in history by a series of secret societies or sects.

Consensus building

A second function of interest groups to seek wider support and allies through persuasion—that is, consensus building for

[4] See Gabriel A. Almond and G. B Powell, Jr., *Comparative Politics* (1966).

the particular interest. On occasion this may be an attempt to win very broad, popular support. In 1970, for example, the Postal Workers Union was able to use the wildcat strike to dramatize how low the wages of postal workers were in comparison with the wages of others, such as the sanitation workers in big cities, and it was quite successful. This public support, in turn, was useful as a pressure on the government in subsequent negotiations.

At other times the consensus-building function is largely one of lobbying on Capitol Hill. The popular image is one of the interest groups buttonholing congressmen with threats of retaliation at the polls, but as mentioned previously, interest groups can only rarely make good any such threat, and congressmen know it. As a consequence, most interest groups do not even bother attempting to persuade known opponents of their view, but concentrate on those who are undecided and on helping those who are known sympathizers. In terms of both time spent and influence achieved, it is this latter activity that is the most important. As the authors of a ten-year study of the making of foreign trade policy say, "To many a Congressman, the interest organization is a source of information about the attitudes of significant groups in his public, a source of research data and speech material, and an unofficial propaganda ally to help him put his own case forward."[5]

Sources of interest group power

If the interest groups can only rarely and in special circumstances deliver the vote of their membership, what is the source of their power? The fact that in certain special circumstances the interest groups *can* deliver a vote—the fact that the potential for retaliation is present—should not be discounted. But beyond this, the major source of their power seems to be "legitimacy"—the expectation among the participants in the policy-making process that there will be re-

---

[5] Bauer, de Sola Pool, and Dexter, *American Business and Public Policy* (1963).

ciprocity among participants, that the purpose of the whole policy-making system is to balance out and satisfy needs, that those who have a legitimate interest have a right to be heard, that in fairness they *should* be heard, and that in fairness their views *should* have weight. V. O. Key goes so far as to argue that the results would be the same even if there were no elections to constitute the ultimate pay-off or ultimate opportunity for retribution, that the interest groups are heard because it is part of the "rules of the game." In any case it is a demonstrable research finding that groups with legitimate interests are heard and do have influence and that by and large they have more influence on matters in which they have a legitimate interest and less influence on matters in which their interest is only peripheral. It is clear, for example, that the influence a labor union is able to exert on labor legislation is considerably greater than what it is able to exert on, say, policy toward the Soviet Union.

THE PRESS

It is no accident that the press, which includes television, is often referred to as the "fourth branch of government." Although it is not provided for in the Constitution, the press plays a vital role in the governmental process.[6]

Most of the large daily newspapers have a number of reporters in Washington concentrating on the White House, the Congress, the Pentagon, and the State Department, and the giants, like the *New York Times,* have at least one reporter for each. This is also true of the radio and television networks. Both the networks and the large daily newspapers also have reporters regularly assigned to the United Nations, as well as

[6] The most comprehensive scholarly work on the press in foreign policy is by Bernard C. Cohen, *The Press and Foreign Policy* (1963). Another, written about the foreign correspondent himself is John Hohenberg's *Foreign Correspondents: The Great Reporters and Their Times,* New York (1964). Others are Douglas Cater, *The Fourth Branch of Government* (1959), and James Reston, *The Artillery of the Press: Its Influence on American Foreign Policy,* New York (1967).

a large body of foreign correspondents who cover every major capital in the world.

Functions of the press

What functions do all these people perform in the making of foreign policy? One, of course, is similar to that of the intelligence organizations—the gathering and dissemination of information. An American correspondent in a foreign capital must, of course, rely on public announcements by the local government for much of his information and on briefings by the staff of the American embassy for a lot more. As a result much of what he reports is not new to Washington officials. But foreign correspondents are able to gather information on their own, and what they do gather is useful. So also is their independent judgment and interpretation of events. Wise Washington officials will always welcome the opportunity to hear an independent opinion to compare with the opinion forwarded by the embassy, even though they may not agree with it. Throughout the Vietnam struggle, for example, the views of the reporters who were critical of the Saigon regime and the American effort in Vietnam were valued by at least some of the officials in Washington as an antidote to the sometimes excessive optimism coming through official channels. In these circumstances the press constitutes a *competing* source of judgment and interpretation.

Another kind of information useful to Washington officials and that is provided by the newspapers and other media is, paradoxically, what is going on in Washington. Congressmen read to find out what is going on in the Executive branch— and sometimes to find out what is going on in other parts of the Congress—so that they can make their own efforts more effective. Officials in the Executive branch read to find out what is going on in both the Congress and elsewhere in the Executive branch. Especially important is information on congressional attitudes. What this senator feels about that bill can often be found in the newspapers, and it is useful to an official as a guide to determining how much effort will have to be made in building public and additional congressional support, for example. Such information is also relevant to hundreds of decisions on tactics, shading, and various compromises along the way. President Eisenhower once remarked that the only newspaper he read was the "News of the Week in Review" in the Sunday *New York Times,* implying that he got more and better information through government channels. Perhaps he did, but his remark was the source of many a political wisecrack, for it indicated to old Washington hands that he was denying himself the information on people in Washington that would be essential to a President who wanted to put through a program of his own. Without that kind of information it seemed likely that President Eisenhower would reign, but not rule.

Interest articulation and interpretation

A second function performed by newspapers, television, and radio is much the same as the major function of the interest groups—interest articulation and interpretation. It might even be said that the press often performs the role of interest group for the unorganized attentive publics. Certainly Washington officials read newspapers for the purpose of ascertaining the mood and reaction of the attentive publics. John F. Kennedy, for example, read five or six newspapers every day. Quite obviously his purpose in reading so many was not to get the basic information in the stories—many of the stories were telling what *he* and his Administration were doing, and for the stories of other kinds, one good newspaper would have sufficed. What he was so interested in was the way the different newspapers "played" the story. During the Laos crisis, for example, the Communist side violated the cease fire, and Kennedy decided on a number of moves, including the movement of the Seventh Fleet to the Gulf of Siam to show the Communists that we would not tolerate their sabotaging the Geneva agreements neutralizing Laos. The *New York Times* play of the story downgraded its significance, implying that the movement of the fleet was a meaningless "show of force" and nothing more. Kennedy was furious for two reasons. The first was that the press play eroded his support for the policy of neutralizing Laos in both the hard-line and soft-line factions in the public, in Congress, and within the Executive branch itself. The play would lead a hard liner to think him soft, and at the same time lead the soft liners to think he was lessening his commitment to the policy of neutralization, which they favored. The second reason was that the play tended to nullify the effect he had intended the move to have on the Communists.

The point here is that the press play will affect the reaction of attentive publics, and an official is better able to predict that reaction by knowing the play. In effect the press is interpreting information in terms of the values and interests of its readers in the same way that an interest group does for its membership. The difference is that with the interest group the emphasis is on the upward function of expressing values and interests to the central decision makers, while with the press the emphasis is on the downward interpretation of how decisions will affect values and interests. But it should be noticed that the press also performs the upward function as well, by the kinds of stories it reports, the kinds of questions it asks, and by its stories on mass and public reaction.

The power of the press

That the press has power, no one questions, but as with the power of the other participants in the policy-making process, the power of the press is difficult to define precisely. It is sometimes assumed that the press and other media can dictate public opinion, in effect control men's minds. Election data make it clear, however, that people do not always vote the way their newspapers tell them to, and poll data make it clear that they do not think the way newspapers tell them to either. At this level, the level of the editorials, the newspapers and other media have only the power to persuade, and in this they must compete with all the others who can command a platform or a printed page, whether officials or private citizens with some claim to expertise or authority.

Quite clearly the press has unusual power to place issues it chooses to emphasize higher on the agenda for action. By reporting a certain issue heavily, the press can focus attention on it and bring enormous pressure to bear on government officials to take action. An example is the familiar one of a newspaper creating a "crime wave" by reporting events they would normally ignore. A decision by the editors of the *New York Times* to report every conceivable incident indicating difficulties in, say, Philippine-American relations would undoubtedly force U.S. government officials to take some action and sooner than they would ordinarily have done.

Notice, however, that this power of the press to focus attention on an issue can be used in certain circumstances by people who are not members of the press. Bernard C. Cohen, for example, likens the press to a musical instrument. "The most successful public relations," he writes, "have generally been the work of people who understood the instrument-like variability of the press and who shared the expert newsman's intuitive ability to define what is 'news' in any situation." An ambitious politician can play on the press if he understands that it "is not simply an automatic transmission belt which can be counted on to carry 'all' information, but rather that newspapermen often have to make judgments and choices as to the significance of information and the emphasis to be placed on it, and that these judgments can be directed or influenced in various ways." As Cohen says, during Senator Joseph McCarthy's witch hunt, thoughtful newsmen were beginning to be uncomfortably aware of the part they had unintentionally played in McCarthy's rapid political rise.

This same power to focus attention on an issue will in certain circumstances give the press the power to kill a planned move by the government by merely publicizing it. At the time of the Bay of Pigs fiasco, for example, the *New York Times* learned of the planned invasion of the Cuban brigade under the sponsorship of the CIA, but President Kennedy telephoned the publisher and asked the *Times* not to print the story. Later he observed regretfully that it would have been better if they had, for the invasion would have had to be canceled if Castro was warned of it by stories in the newspapers. As a practical matter, however, the news media will be extremely careful in publishing information of this kind. Consider what would have happened if the *Times* had published the story and the invasion had in fact been canceled. The *Times* would not have gotten credit for preventing a disaster, but for wrecking a victory. They would have been blamed for permitting Castro to defeat the anti-Communist Cubans without having fired a shot, for giving secret information to the enemy—in short, for treason. The *Times* had the power to bring about the cancellation of the invasion, yes, but the cost for doing so would have been very high indeed.

The power to interpret events

Probably the most important source of the power of the press in making foreign policy is that it is a principal source of the *interpretation* of events. Thus the press is one of the main architects of the structure of whatever debate takes place on the policy that the United States should pursue in dealing with those events.

Here again, the press is not the sole source of interpretation. The President, the secretary of state, the assistant secretaries, American ambassadors, senators, congressmen, academic experts—all are sources of interpretation. But the fact that the press is there every day, day after day, with its interpretations makes it the principal competitor of all the others in interpreting events. It forces officials who advocate a particular policy that differs in some way from what flows from the interpretation given by the press to compete actively, to make public speeches, to hold press conferences—to do everything they can to get *their* interpretation in the same headlines the press interpretation of events automatically achieves.

Interpretation comes not just in the places where it is clearly labeled interpretation—that is, in the writings of the columnists like Walter Lippmann, James Reston, Joe Kraft, and Joseph Alsop. It also occurs in the news pages, in the facts that are selected for reporting, in the way those facts are arranged—in what might be called the *implied* interpretation. In the spring of 1968, for example, the press largely played the news of the Tet offensive in Vietnam very dramatically, suggesting that the Viet Cong could strike anywhere in Vietnam almost at will, that the defenses were weak, and that the optimism that had come from the American embassy, the military headquarters, and Washington had been exposed as false. The Johnson Administration, on the other hand, interpreted the offensive as "a desperate last gasp" of a defeated enemy, as a total failure resulting in prohibitive casualties for the Communist side and as the prelude to an imminent collapse of the enemy effort. It was vitally important to the Johnson Administration which interpretation was to win the struggle for general acceptance. If the enemy was virtually defeated and victory a matter of only a few more months of cleaning up, public and congressional support for the war effort could undoubtedly be sustained. But if the Viet Cong were in fact stronger than ever, as suggested in the press interpretation, and the war would have to go on for a long time at even higher levels of violence and sacrifice, then public and congressional support would almost immediately collapse. With the benefit of hindsight it can be argued that both interpretations were oversimplifications, but the fact is that in the end it was the interpretation offered by the press that prevailed and not that offered by the President, the secretary of state, and the other members of the Johnson Administration. The result was what we have described before: even more people moved into opposition on Vietnam and President Johnson felt that his only course was to stop the bombing of North Vietnam, begin negotiations in Paris, and—to make the change in policy credible and effective—to withdraw as a candidate for reelection as President. In such circumstances as the Tet offensive in 1968, the mere opportunity to compete with the government in interpreting events makes for power to influence policy that is nothing less than awesome.

SEVEN
POLICY MAKING AS
A POLITICAL PROCESS

P OLICY making is a political process. When decisions are made on the big questions, questions requiring sacrifices by the nation or concentrating on one set of objectives at the cost of neglecting others, there is struggle and conflict. At the same time, there is a "strain toward agreement,"[1] an effort to build a consensus, a push for accommodation, for compromise, for some sort of agreement on the policy decision. There are independent participants in the process who may be able to block a policy, or sabotage it, or at least to snipe away at it from the sidelines. There may be other men whose active, imaginative support and dedicated efforts are required if the policy is to succeed, and it may take concessions aimed directly at them and their interests to enlist this kind of willing cooperation. Finally there is in all participants an intuitive realization that prolonged intransigence, stalemate, and indecision on urgent and fundamental issues might become so intolerable as to threaten the very form and structure of the system of governance.

To recapitulate the argument so far, the great fallacy

[1] The phrase is Warner R. Schilling's. See his "The Politics of National Defense: Fiscal 1950," in Schilling, Hammond, and Snyder, *Strategy, Politics, and Defense Budgets* (1962). p. 23.

in the Wilsonian ideal was to suppose that all the electorate would be equally interested in all subjects and acquire the specialized information and knowledge to choose intelligently among the alternatives. But when the interests of political scientists turned to empirical work, it quickly became clear that different segments of the public were interested in different things—that there is not one public, but many. Within the general public, there is a division of labor—one attentive public for agricultural policy, another for Latin American affairs, and perhaps still another for policy toward Asia. Informed and interested groups follow each policy area, but the general public becomes involved in a particular policy only rarely. Ending the Korean War became a major issue in the election of 1952, for example, and thus engaged the general public. But war touches all our lives, and examples of foreign policy issues that directly influenced the outcome of an election are few.[2]

THE CONCENTRIC RINGS OF POLICY MAKING

Approached from the other direction, from the Washington end, the policy-making process presents itself as a series of concentric circles.[3] The innermost circle, of course, is the President and the men in the different departments and agen-

[2] Even if foreign policy *issues* do not seem to play a very important part in elections, the electorate apparently wants its candidates for national office to have qualifications or experience that show *competency* in foreign affairs. See Angus Campbell, and others, *The American Voter* (1960, 1964).
[3] The theoretical model of the policy-making process that follows owes much to the work of Gabriel A. Almond, especially his *The American People and Foreign Policy*. An earlier attempt at this model—influenced not only by Almond, but also by Charles E. Lindblom's article, "The Science of 'Muddling Through,' " and the works of Robert A. Dahl—is contained in my 1958 and 1959 articles, "Congressional-Executive Relations and the Foreign Policy Consensus," and "The Foreign Policy Consensus: An Interim Research Report." The model as presented here draws on the subsequent work of Warner R. Schilling, "The Politics of National Defense," *loc. cit.;* Samuel P. Huntington, *The Common Defense* (1960); and Thomas Schelling, *The Strategy of Conflict* (1960), as well as the later work of Almond, Dahl, and Lindblom.

cies who must carry out the decision—staff men in the White House, the secretaries of state and defense, the director of the CIA, and the assistant secretaries of state and defense who bear responsibility for whatever the particular problem may be. Some matters never go beyond this circle, but even here the process is political—the "closed politics" of highly secret decision making.[4] President Truman had to consider the political effect of General MacArthur's opposition when he made decisions during the Korean War, such as the decision not to bomb north of the Yalu. President Eisenhower had to consider the political effects of the Army's opposition to his decision to adopt a strategy of "massive retaliation" which relied mainly on the Air Force. President Kennedy had to consider the political effect of the opposition of the hard-line "Cold Warriors" when he decided on the neutralization of Laos in the Geneva conference of 1962. President Johnson had to consider the political effects of the "doves" in the Executive branch when he decided to escalate the war in Vietnam, some of whom later resigned and opposed his policies in public.

Beyond this innermost circle lie other departments of the Executive branch and other layers within the agencies and departments already involved, including Presidential commissions, scientific advisory panels, and so on. Even though the debate might still remain secret from the press, the Congress, and the public, these second layers soon become involved. In the Laos crisis of 1962, for example, the debate over whether or not to send American troops directly into Laos from Thailand continued for weeks. It was all still top secret, but more and more people became involved in the closed politics of the decision. Specialists in the State Department's Bureau of Intelligence and Research and in the Policy Planning Staff and similar specialists in the CIA and the Defense Department became aware of the debate and pushed forward additional information in their province of responsibility that bore on the subject or wrote memoranda that might have an

[4] The phrase is C. P. Snow's. See his *Science and Government* (1960, 1961).

influence one way or another. People in the RAND Corporation learned of the struggle and rushed copies of their study of the logistical capacity of the transportation routes in Laos to people they knew would use it to good advantage. The longer a policy debate goes on, no matter how delicate the issue is, the larger the number of people who become involved, until eventually the debate spills over into the public domain. It is for this reason that there is sometimes an incentive to avoid "forward thinking" or any other form of contingency planning. For example, Secretary Rusk, in that same Laos crisis of 1962, wished to avoid even asking the President for a decision about whether or not we would order American forces into Laos if the Communists continued their nibbling tactics. No decision need be made until the Communists actually moved, and the Secretary of State argued that the President ought not to make the decision in advance. If he decided that the United States should *not* intervene and the Communist side learned of the decision, they would be encouraged to go ahead. If he decided that the United States *should* intervene and word got out, on the other hand, the public debate would inevitably become an obstacle to swift and effective action. But if there were no decision in advance, there would be nothing to leak.

The public arena

The next arena is the public one, involving Congress, the press, interest groups, and inevitably, the attentive publics. In this arena a decision on policy may be made in any one of several ways. The Cuban missile crisis became public, but it never did enter the public arena for decision. The decision was made in the arena of closed politics, and although the President had always to consider the effects and reactions and repercussions in the wider public arena, the crisis moved too fast for a public debate to catch up. Policy toward Indonesia during the confrontation with Malaysia became public in a variety of ways, focused especially through Congress's authority over appropriations, but it remained the province only of those very few in the Congress, the press, and so on who had already had a developed interest. Important though understanding the emerging nations might be in the long run, for most Americans the problem of Indonesia remained esoteric. Like blue cheese, it was an acquired taste.

In the Congo crisis, in Laos, in China policy, in Vietnam—in all these a wide variety of people became involved in one way or another. The debate over Vietnam, to cite the most vivid example, took place in the National Security Council, in the halls of Congress, in the press, in academic journals, inside the United States Mission in Vietnam, within each of the departments and agencies of the Executive branch in Washington, and so on and on. The battle lines were drawn between the State Department and the Defense Department, but alliances also cut straight across the institutional boundaries. Individual members of the embassy and of the CIA shared the views of a segment of the press, while other members of the embassy and CIA were allied with the opposing segment of the press. Some members of Congress shared the view of a group in the State Department, opposed by other members of Congress allied with others in the Executive branch. Inevitably the activities of a group in one institution supported the activities of its allies in the other, with or without any attempt at connivance. In Saigon the "hawks" leaked to hawkish members of the press; the "doves" leaked to dovish members of the press. In Washington, hawkish senators put up resolutions supporting the "hawks" in the State Department; dovish senators put up resolutions supporting the "doves"—even when the different factions did not ask for supporting resolutions and even when they felt obliged to urge the senators to hold back.

There was also the "strain toward agreement"—the effort to reach a consensus, to work out a compromise, to enlist the support of others standing at the edge of the debate. Considering the depth of the disagreement in some of the problems previously mentioned—Laos, Vietnam, Cuba, and the Congo, for example—the remarkable thing is not that there was conflict, but that there was sufficient accommodation to make a decision possible. And the extent of accommodation and consensus would probably look even more remarkable if the other great issues of foreign policy since World War II were considered—the Marshall Plan, NATO and the containment of the Soviet Union, and the bitter interservice quarrels over weapons and military strategy.

CHARACTERISTICS AND CONSEQUENCES OF THE SYSTEM

The fact that policy is made through a political process of conflict and consensus building accounts for much of the untidiness and turmoil on the Washington scene. The issues are important. There are rival policies for dealing with them, and the rival policies are sponsored by different groups of advocates competing for the approval or support of a variety of different constituencies. Attracting the attention of such varied audiences requires something dramatic. It takes effort and many comings and goings to enlist allies and forestall opponents. A high noise level is a natural consequence of the system itself.

The leak

Consider, for example, the seemingly endless leaks of secret information. Many are not leaks at all. Sometimes a leak is really a trial balloon, launched anonymously in a "background" press conference to test the possibility of building a consensus without the penalty of making a fullscale attempt and failing.

Sometimes information leaks, not because the policy makers want it to, but because the press drills a hole. There is a deeply idealistic conviction in the Washington press corps that newsmen have a duty to inform the wider public of what the government is doing.[5] A selfish interest is added by the fact that conflict and disagreement within the government

[5] See Bernard C. Cohen, *The Press and Foreign Policy* (1963).

put official stories on the front page. Finally, there are always some in the press who are just as passionately committed to a particular policy view as any of the officials inside the government and just as anxious to influence the policy decisions.

All these are high incentives, and many a leak is just hard digging by diligent and dedicated reporters. A particularly vivid example occurred in the wake of the Cuban missile crisis, when there were so many charges of "managing the news" that both the press and the policy makers were a little touchy. There had been an exchange of cables in which Premier Khrushchev had finally made a concession on withdrawing troops. Just about this time, a reporter from the *New York Times* and one from the *Washington Post* cornered Mc-George Bundy at a reception and pushed him hard about "news management." Irritated, Bundy said that he knew something that would sooner or later be released and that it would make a big headline, but that the press would *not* be told until the government was good and ready. The two reporters were equally irritated, and each went back to his office and called in as many of his colleagues as he could reach. After talking it over, each group developed two or three ideas about what it might be that Bundy was holding back, and the possibility that it might be a cable from Khrushchev about something to do with Cuba was naturally on both lists. Each set of reporters began to make telephone calls, asking officials if it was true that the cable from Khrushchev had said thus and so, trying a different idea each time. "Oh, no, no, no," one or another official would say, falling into the trap. "It wasn't like that at all." By the time several different officials had "corrected" what would have been a damaging story, both sets of reporters had full and accurate accounts of what was in the cable.

Many leaks are of this order. Some others are sheer accident. But then there are true leaks, deliberate and knowing. Even these are not really blabbermouthed irresponsibility, but more often attempts by men who are deeply convinced, rightly or wrongly, that their cause is overwhelmingly just. They believe that they have both the right and the duty, if their inside effort has failed, to use the public channel, to force an issue or policy alternative up to the level of decision, to outflank the proponents of a rival view, or to appeal a decision to a higher tribunal and a wider public. And they will have sympathetic encouragement from allies in both the press and the Congress.

The oversimplification of the policy debate

The fact that policy is made in a political process of conflict and consensus building also accounts for some of the other apparent absurdities of the Washington scene. Often the public debate on foreign policy is childishly oversimplified, for example. The problem of Sukarno and Indonesia was far more complicated than Congressman Broomfield pictured it when he called Sukarno a "Hitler," and the problem of Tshombe and the secession of Katanga was not just a question of the "good guys" versus the "bad guys" as Senator Dodd's speeches implied. Both Broomfield and Dodd probably understood this as well as anyone else, but if the debate is taking place in front of a variety of audiences whose attention is easily diverted, then the alternatives must be very clear-cut, simple, dramatic, and the arguments painted in colors that are both bold and bright.

Another consequence of the multiplicity of constituencies involved in policy making is that more and more problems are thrown into the White House. It is only the Presidency— the President himself, his immediate aides in the White House, or *his* men in the departments and agencies—who can consider the whole broad range of interconnections between conflicting interests and demands. Judging these interconnections from the point of view of the President requires someone who partakes of the pressures *on* the President— facing Congress, the press, and the demanding interest groups —and who has his own future tied to the President and his administration. It was only the President himself or someone who identified with him rather than the particular department or agency in which he served, for example, who could ask, as President Kennedy so often asked, "How can we justify fighting a war with American troops in Southeast Asia, which is nine thousand miles away, when we can't justify it in Cuba, which is only ninety miles away?"

All this means that competition for attention at the decision-making level of government becomes more intense. Before a new problem or proposal can be raised to the level of decision, it must jostle out hundreds of others. What might be called the "jurisdictional" effect of bureaucracy tends to increase still more the number of problems that must elbow their way right to the very top. The essence of bureaucracy is specialization of function and a division of labor and responsibility accordingly. This device is indispensable in managing large-scale enterprises, but it presents peculiar difficulties when it comes time to fix responsibility for problems that cut across jurisdictional lines, which foreign policy problems tend to do in any age and especially so in time of external threat when both military and economic instrumentalities are prominent. More often than not, complex problems arising out of interaction, as between military and political considerations, can be "recognized" as problems in an official sense only at the top. The heart of the problem of guerrilla warfare, for example, lies at the intersection of political and military factors. No one department or agency can begin to cope, and the whole problem can be faced only at the level of the Presidency. Since the solution is the same mixture, carrying out the policy in the field requires the same type of overall authority—presenting a problem in implementation for which the American form of government is ill-equipped.

A policy-making system that revolves around developing a consensus among a wide range of participants also puts a high premium on effective communication and an even higher penalty on a failure of communication. Many a policy maker has been defeated mainly because he neglected to communicate effectively to the Washington constituencies that might have been his allies what it was he was trying to do and why. Achieving sophisticated policies is not just a problem of policy planning by an elite staff, but also one of persuading and educating. What is more, there seems to be no one place where these tasks can be accomplished fully, since there are too many participants too widely scattered to be reached by the communications resources available to any one group of participants, including probably those available to the White House itself.

The need for wide support sometimes leads to overselling a policy proposal in the sense of claiming too much for it. This happened to some extent in the case of Kennedy's policy of neutralizing Laos, and somewhat more in his justification of giving aid and advisers to Vietnam. For President Johnson's policy of escalation in Vietnam, it was devastating. But the classic example would be the foreign aid program as a whole. Foreign aid was supposed to create military allies and at the same time ensure democratic regimes as economic development was achieved. Both these claims created false expectations at home that eventually eroded support for foreign aid not only among conservatives but among the very liberals who were the most ardent backers of the aid program.

Paradoxically the need for wide support for a foreign policy sometimes creates an incentive *not* to communicate effectively, to be a little fuzzy in articulating policy and its possible outcomes. Different groups climb aboard a particular policy for different reasons, sometimes because of a differing estimate of just what the true outcome of a policy will be. The politician in a President has a need at times to postpone a decision until there is time to build a consensus, or to proceed in painfully slow increments for the same reason. Every President has occasionally been accused of obfuscation and indecisiveness. Some of Lincoln's Cabinet members despaired of getting a decision from him, and similar incidents are told of both Roosevelts, Wilson, and the other Presidents with a reputation for strength and decisiveness. As an executive and the leader of a large and complicated organization, the President needs to be articulate and precise; as a politician, he may need to be vague. Inevitably there is tension between the two.

The effort that must go into selling a policy that requires wide support, the tension between the need for articulation and the need for fuzziness, the difficulty in getting some kinds of problems "recognized" except at the top, and the competition for the attention of the many constituencies and levels of government all combine to put obstacles in the way of any attempt at systematic policy making. Some issues or proposals are the subject of massive concentration, while others are neglected almost entirely. There is a tendency to bounce from the crest of one crisis to the crest of another, and a bias toward postponing final choice among the possible alternatives until the new crisis forces decisions that are mainly reactions, the children of events rather than their master. Because so many different people and so many different constituencies are involved, it takes the urgency of crisis to force attention and point up the necessity for the mutual concessions and accommodation out of which consensus on a policy is reached.

Incrementalism

There is also a tendency to decide as little as possible.[6] Partly this is because of the impossibility, as Charles E. Lindblom has pointed out, of giving rational consideration to the whole wide range of goals and the multiplicity of alternative means for achieving them and calculating the myriad of consequences and interactions.[7] Policy, as Lindblom says, tends to proceed in a series of incremental steps, tentative and easily reversible. It seems clear that this is true, not only because of the impossibility of analyzing the grand alternatives ra-

[6] On this point, see Warner R. Schilling, "The H-Bomb Decision: How to Decide Without Actually Choosing," *Political Science Quarterly* (March 1961).

[7] Charles E. Lindblom, *The Intelligence of Democracy*, chap. 9.

tionally, but also because of the political process of consensus building by which policy is made. The acquiescence of a key constituency might be given for what could be regarded as a tentative, reversible experiment when it would be withheld for a grand leap.

All of this—the bouncing from crisis to crisis, the overselling, the incrementalism—leads to what might be called a discontinuity of policy development. There are gaps in both analysis and policy as a result of the working of the system itself. The Sino-Soviet dispute showed that the Communist world was not the monolith it was supposed to be, but policy based on the assumption that it was a monolith continued through the sheer inertia of the process itself. Guerrilla warware showed the inadequacy of strategic thinking, but a massive conventional military effort continued to dominate strategy in Vietnam long after a more sophisticated concept had been worked out. Americans feel that they have been too often surprised by the turn of international events, and they tend to blame the intelligence agencies on whom, they feel, so much effort has been lavished to what seems so little avail. But the real reason for their being surprised seems more likely to be here, in the discontinuities growing out of the very nature of the policy-making process.

ADVANTAGES OF THE PROCESS

In spite of the untidiness and turmoil of the politics of policy making in Washington, such an open process of conflict and consensus building, debate, assessment, and mutual adjustment and accommodation can be solidly effective in the assessment of broad policy alternatives if the conditions are right. The conditions are, first, that the subject is one on which the competing groups of advocates are knowledgeable. Second, both the participating constituencies within the government and the attentive publics outside must be well informed. Third, all levels of government, those who will carry out the policy as well as those who decide it, must be responsive to the decision and persuaded by it. Under these conditions the chances are good that the policy will be wise, that the effort and sacrifice required will be forthcoming, and that the work of carrying out the policy will go forward intelligently and energetically. An example is the development of United States policy toward Europe in the years following World War II—the broad policy highlighted by the Truman doctrine, the Marshall Plan, and the establishment of NATO —which successfully halted the slide of western Europe into Soviet domination and eventually helped to bring it to security and prosperity. The advocates of rival policies, the constituencies inside the government, and the attentive publics outside were equipped with a frame of knowledge about Europe and its problems aaginst which to test proposed policies, and the results were good.

An example of the opposite is the story of China policy, which for so long lacked the necessary frame of knowledge for intelligent debate at every level, within the government and outside it. Even the Assistant Secretary of State for Far Eastern Affairs at the time, Dean Rusk, could argue that the Chinese Communist regime might be a "colonial Russian government' but that it was "not Chinese." China policy also illustrates how a doctrinaire rigidity can take over and substitute for a frame of knowledge. The Committee of One Million, which was the official name of the so-called China Lobby, and its allies in Congress and the press, for example, were still insisting that communism was a "passing phase" on the mainland long after an ordinary citizen would have taken the common sense view that the Communists had been in control too long to be considered merely a passing phase even if they were successfully ousted.

Interestingly enough, the point seems to hold even when the needs of secrecy and speed keep the process circumscribed—when the decision is made in a process of closed politics rather than open. In the Cuban missile crisis the number of participants was small, but the frame of knowledge was there, the alternative views were expressed, the debate was wide ranging, and the presence of competing interests and the wider implications were felt even though the representation was limited. One has the impression, for example, that the President decided against an air strike in his own mind almost immediately, that the long discussion of it over the next few days was to try to bring the "hawks" around and, failing that, at least to have the record show that their alternative was given a full and complete hearing. The result was a policy decision that not only was successful, but seems as wise under the scrutiny of hindsight as it did at the time.

The obvious example from the Kennedy Administration of a decision made in closed politics that suffered from an inadequate frame of knowledge was, of course, the Bay of Pigs. But what is worth pondering is that, unlike the case of China policy, the necessary knowledge was in fact available in Washington. The trouble was different. In the Cuban missile crisis the demands for secrecy kept the number of participants small, but all the different viewpoints, constituencies, and centers of expertise were still represented. In the Bay of Pigs decision, however, secrecy resulted in the exclusion not only of rival advocates but also of centers of expertise and prevented debate before the full range of governmental constituencies.

EIGHT
THE NATURE
OF POLITICS

I F policy making is a political process, what can be said about political processes in general? The first thing to be said is probably that they are similar to one another—that decision making in Washington in many ways resembles decision making not only in London, Paris, and Rome, but also in Moscow, Peking, and Hanoi. In each of these capitals, different factions struggle for support among a variety of different power centers within the particular society. The number of actors with independent power might differ, and this difference might have profound repercussions for the life of the individual. The rival power centers, for example, might consist only of the party, the military, and the secret police with no role for interest groups or the attentive publics at all. But the *process* of conflict and consensus building seems to be the same, that is, policy appears to be made in a political process.

Decision making at the national level also seems to be similar to that at the international level, that is, a process of conflict and consensus building.[1] In international affairs the principal mode of conflict is war, and people thus tend to assume that conflict between nations is funda-

[1] Others who have commented on the parallel between domestic and international politics are Nicholas John Spykman, W. T. R. Fox, and Warner Schilling.

mentally different from the conflict within a single country or in private lives. Yet even in the "total" wars of recent times, the use of force is limited. Mankind uses force against some natural enemies with the full intention of exterminating them, as the wolves in England were exterminated or the snakes in Ireland. But except for Hitler's maniacal policy toward the Jews, no modern nation has deliberately set about to destroy another people. Physical violence, in fact, is not really a very common state of affairs between nations. In the history of most nations the years of peace far outnumber the years of war. Even when conflict is the dominating theme in a set of relationships, statecraft is not really concerned as much with physical violence, the military art, as it is with threats of physical violence, or still more accurately with manipulating all the varied forms of power—since physical violence is only one of several means that nations use to coerce or influence one another.

It is on the conflict in international affairs that a pure power theory of world politics focuses. Yet for all its utility in explaining the maneuverings of states, a pure power theory has limitations. Without a sizable list of inelegant qualifications, it cannot account for the long periods of peace in international relations, for the stability of certain friendships, and for the not uncommon occasions when nations knowingly relinquish positions of power. For the practical purposes of estimating the consequences of different policies and so of choosing between them, a pure power theory of politics is a cumbersome and uneconomic tool.

The difficulty comes from the multipliicty of values shared by people on both sides of national boundaries—peace, security, prosperity, self-determination, and the sanctity and freedom of the individual. Thus one nation's gain is not always another's loss, and accommodation and concerted action occur almost as frequently in international affairs as conflict.[2]

---

[2] For descriptions of international politics in which both conflict and accommodation appear, see the following among others: Nicholas John Spykman, W. T. R. Fox, Hans J. Morgenthau, Arnold Wolfers, and Thomas Schelling.

The obvious example of nations acting in concert are alliances for security against a common enemy, but nations also act in concert for a variety of lesser purposes—to regulate trade, to counter economic depressions, to conserve such natural resources as fisheries, to combat crime, and to provide international postal and other services.

There is accommodation between adversaries, too. Rival nations often agree, formally or tacitly, to respect spheres of exclusive influence, to act together in neutralizing a third country, or to refrain from bringing certain matters into the arena of competition. The bitterest rivals have a stake in restricting their competition to means that are appropriate to the goals at issue and in avoiding measures that will bring about the sacrifice of things more cherished than those to be won. Even nations at war have reached agreements. Gas was outlawed in World War II, although not all the participants had signed the convention on the rules of war. In the Korean War there was a tacit agreement to respect sanctuaries. The United Nations forces refrained from bombing north of the Yalu and the Communist forces conformed by avoiding Pusan and our bases in Japan. In Vietnam there was until 1965 a tacit agreement that the United States would refrain from bombing North Vietnam and the North Vietnamese would refrain from infiltrating their regular battalions into the South.

Thus international politics has a mixture of conflict and accommodation similar to that in domestic politics. As a consequence, the business between nations, like the business of reaching decisions within a single nation, requires techniques for persuasion, negotiation, and bargaining, as well as for manipulating power.

The practitioners of statecraft, the operators in foreign offices and embassies do not make a practice of generalizing about the "decision-making procedures of world politics" or the "international decision-making system." Neither do they comment on the resemblance between international politics and a process of consensus building. Yet faced with the problem of *doing* something in international affairs—whether it is trying to bring about a Geneva conference on Laos or implementing a decision to blockade Cuba—any practitioner, from desk officer to assistant secretary, would unerringly tick off the steps to be taken. Nation A would have to be consulted in advance; nations B and C would have only to be informed. *This* line of argument should be taken in the UN, *that* line of argument with the press. Moscow should be told *this* at *that* stage; Paris should be handled in a different way. Practitioners may not generalize about the "international decision-making system," but they know how to operate it.

THE DEFINITION OF POLITICS

How one defines politics depends very much on what analytical purposes one has in mind. Politics has been defined as the struggle to determine "who gets what, when, and how" for one analytical purpose.[3] It has been defined as a struggle for power, pure and simple, for other purposes.[4] And there are still many other definitions.[5] Most of them are reasonably valid and useful for particular purposes, and most of them are not completely satisfactory for all purposes. It is probably not necessary to strain for the perfect definition. Most people have a common sense definition that is good enough. People speak of "office politics," for example, and everyone

[3] Harold Lasswell, *Politics: Who Gets What, When, How,* 1958.
[4] Charles E. Merriam, *Political Power: Its Composition and Incidence,* 1934; Hans J. Morgenthau, *Politics Among Nations.*
[5] Although they by no means exhaust the list, three others might be noted here. First, is V. O. Key's definition of politics as the "human relationship of superordination and subordination, of dominance and submission, of the governors and the governed" (*Politics, Parties and Pressure Groups,* 4th ed. 1958). Second is David Easton's definition of politics as the making and executing of the "authoritative," that is, legally binding, decisions in a society (*The Political System,* 1953, and "An Approach to the Analysis of Political Systems," *World Politics,* April 1957). Third is Gabriel A. Almond's as "that system of interactions to be found in all independant societies which performs the functions of integration and adaption (both internally and vis-à-vis other societies) by means of the employment, or threat of employment, of more or less legitimate physical violence" (*The Politics of Developing Areas,* 1960).

knows what they mean. As a general rule, people assume that politics is concerned with power, that it is more likely than not concerned with matters of government, and that political decisions of the largest moment are concerned with the ordering and regulating of society itself. In its broadest meaning, politics concerns the activities and relationships of groups of people as groups.

Politics as group decision making

For the purposes of analyzing the making of foreign policy, it seems most useful to look at a political process with the latter emphasis—as a device for making group decisions, a procedure by which a group of people can decide what they should do as a group, the goals they should seek and the means for achieving them, or how they should divide among themselves those benefits already available. Politics would be concerned both with the making of such decisions and the maneuvering to acquire the power and influence to affect them.

There are, of course, other devices for the making of group decisions—judicial and administrative procedures, for example, in which decisions are made by the interpretation, guided by precedent, of sets of laws, policies, rules, and regulations, or perhaps by tribal customs.

One can conceive of group decisions made in a purely hierarchical way in which only the head man had a vote. At the other extreme, one could also conceive of a pure type of democratic decision making in which there was no leader at all and decisions were made unanimously or by the majority, with each man really having only one vote and no influence other than his vote. But the real world is more complex. It differs from the pure hierarchical model of decision making in that more than one person has power or influence on decisions and from the pure democratic model in that the participants have differing amounts of power and influence. The active cooperation of some people may be required for a decision, as we have seen, while only the acquiescence of others may be necessary. Some participants might have to give formal approval before some decisions could be made; on other decisions these same people might be safely ignored.

Also several different forms of group decision making might be operative at the same time. Within a single department of the government, some decisions are made by hierarchical procedures, some by judicial, and some by political, and perhaps some by a combination of all three. Not infrequently officials are called upon to play roles appropriate to every possible form of decision making in swift and bewildering succession with few cues as to when the scene is changing.[6]

CHARACTERISTICS OF A POLITICAL PROCESS

Three characteristics distinguish a political process of decision making from other ways of making group decisions. In the first place, politics implies a diversity of goals and values that must be reconciled before a decision can be reached. It is not just a question of whether this or that value should be pursued, but what mixture of values should be pursued. It also implies alternative means for achieving values whose precise effects may be in dispute. There is never a political debate over the tensile strength required for the truss members of a bridge, which can be determined with great exactitude, but there frequently is a political debate over the economic and social effects of locating the bridge at one place on a river rather than another, which cannot be determined with such exactitude.

Frequently a debate over the probable effects of alternative means is really a mask for an unspoken disagreement about goals. In the making of foreign policy, at least, it is noteworthy how often the debate is truly over means and predictions about what a particular means will or will not

[6] On the overlapping of different forms of decision making and the psychological problems posed for the individual, see Robert A. Dahl, "Hierarchy, Democracy, and Bargaining in Politics and Economics," in *Research Frontiers in Politics and Government* (The Brookings Institution, 1955).

accomplish. In the Cuban missile crisis, in the Congo crisis, in China policy, in the Laos crisis, in South Vietnam—in all these there was by and large agreement about the general objective, and the debate was over which means would best accomplish the objective at what risk and at what cost.

Politics, in other words, begins to come to the fore when there is disagreement (1) about the goals the group should seek as a group, or (2) about the effects of alternative means for achieving the goal, or (3) about the rules governing competition between individuals and subgroups, or (4) about the allocation of benefits held or distributed by the group as a whole, or (5) about the sacrifices required by different segments of the group as a whole. It is not competition alone that produces politics. If there is substantial agreement, for example, that unrestrained economic enterprise shall govern the distribution of material benefits, the competition will take place in other than political terms. It is when there is disagreement about the rules for economic competition that politics begins.

A second characteristic of a political process is the presence of competing clusters of people within the main group who are identified with each of these alternative goals and policies. One thinks most readily of the traditional political parties, but even on the national scene there will be other rival groupings—from farmers, labor, management, liberals, conservatives, down to special interests like the National Rifle Association fighting against gun control laws. In the policy-making arena, there are subgroups of many kinds within the Executive branch and even within a single department. Frequently these are entirely informal alliances that cut across departmental or institutional lines, including the lines between the Executive and Congress. Throughout the struggle in Vietnam, for example, there were groups within the State Department who took a "hawk" view, who had friends and allies in the Pentagon, in the CIA, in the Congress, the press, and in the attentive public, while the rival group who took a "dove" view found an entirely different set of allies. This pattern of subgroups and informal alliances runs through each of the major policy disputes, sometimes more and sometimes less prominently.

In a political process, finally, the relative power of the different groups of people involved is as relevant to the final decision as the appeal of the goals they seek or the cogency and wisdom of their arguments. It was the political power that the China Lobby could muster at the height of its influence, and not the persuasiveness of the argument, to cite the most obvious example, that bound policy so tightly for so long. Who advocates a particular policy is as important as what he advocates.

Viewing policy making as a political process in the sense described by these characteristics illuminates the diversity and inconsistency of the goals that national policy must serve, as pointed out in the first chapter of this book, and calls attention to the powerful but sometimes hidden forces through which these competing goals are reconciled. It helps explain, as we said, why the push and pull of these cross-currents are sometimes dampened or obscured and why they are sometimes so fiercely public. The roles of such "un-rational" procedures as bargaining also become more clear.

POLITICAL POWER

A third theoretical comment that might be made here is on the nature of political power as illuminated in the making of United States foreign policy. It seems beyond dispute that power is a factor in any political process. Everyone recognizes the obvious fact that some people have more power than others in every society in the world, and all the great social thinkers have devoted their attention to the nature of power. As Robert A. Dahl has pointed out, the existence of so much comment arouses two suspicions.[7] The first is that where there is so much smoke there must be fire and some

---

[7] Robert A. Dahl, "The Concept of Power, *Behavioral Science* (July 1957).

"Thing" that can be called power must exist. The second suspicion is that "a Thing to which people attach many labels with subtly or grossly different meanings in many different cultures and times is probably not a Thing at all but many Things. . . ."

The sources of power

We have argued that policy making is a political process, and on the face of it power and politics are intertwined. Yet power is a crude concept, as Dahl suggests, and it fails to satisfy as an explanation of the mixture of both conflict and accommodation that is present, of the motives that presumably lie behind the decisions on foreign policy, or of the techniques that are used to achieve agreement or acquiesence on a policy.

If it is correct to say that the peculiar province of politics is matters in which there is disagreement about either group goals and values or the rules of competition and allocation of those individual values and interests that are regulated by the group, then power need not be quite so central in either domestic politics or international. Power need not be the motive force for most participants, nor the cause of politics, nor even a necessary condition, but only one of the more pervasive and perhaps decisive of the several instruments of politics.

At certain times and in certain places, military power, for example, may be starkly central in domestic affairs—civil war is the obvious example. But to the extent that military strength is a *source* of power on the domestic scene, the mechanism is not so crude. In the making of foreign policy there has been a policy view and position from what President Eisenhower called the "military-industrial complex" on some issues, such as arms control and Vietnam, both of which involved a large military stake. In such cases power has clearly been exerted in support of that view and position. But as a force the military-industrial complex has been loosely organized, amorphous, more potential than structured—nothing, certainly, that resembles in the slightest the "power elites" described in Marxist and neo-Marxist literature. During Indonesia's "confrontation" with Malaya in the 1960s, for example, the oil companies had a huge investment in Indonesia, but their inclination was not to push the United States into greater involvement but to get themselves out. More than once it was only because of the urgings of the United States government that American businesses were persuaded to stay in Indonesia as long as they did.

In the domestic scene, clearly, power has more varied and subtle sources than in either force and violence or wealth and class. Power grows not only "out of the barrel of a gun," as Mao Tse-tung would have it, but also in legitimacy, in legal authority, in expertise, and in special interest that is recognized as legitimate, such as the interest of the farmer in agricultural policy or the banker in monetary policy. It is so varied and subtle in its sources, indeed, that one wonders whether "power" is the most useful word.

Power can be the negative power that Congress has of making life difficult for the President if one of its treasured views is ignored. It can be the legal and constitutional right to decide in a formal sense, which is usually the President's in foreign affairs but sometimes belongs to Congress. It can be influence, in the sense of having the ear of the President or the respect of the leaders of Congress without holding any office at all. It can be the ability to have one's views at least taken into account because one represents a special interest group like the farmers, as we said, whose legitimacy is recognized. It can also be the ability to have one's views taken into account simply because one has convinced the world that one speaks for a wider public and that there will be political consequences if one is ignored. An example is Marvin Liebman, who as Executive Secretary of the Committee of One Million could get a hearing because he was accepted as the spokesman for the China Lobby and presumably for a wider public that supported the views of Chiang Kai-shek. It can also be the ability to have one's views taken into account because of one's personal expertise. When George Kennan speaks about policy toward the Soviet Union, for example, the government listens even when it abhors the advice offered and refuses to take it. Power can also come simply because one has a "platform" which gives one the opportunity of enlisting a particular constituency. An Adlai Stevenson or a Chester Bowles out of office can influence policy by his ability to command a hearing before "liberals" and the possibility that he might swing the whole constituency with his persuasiveness. A scientist who is completely unknown outside the scientific community might develop such leverage, and if the subject matter concerned a scientific question, the leverage might be overwhelming. No President would lightly go against the consensus of scientists on a matter in the area of their specialty.

Within the Executive branch itself power comes to some people because they enjoy the confidence of the President. Power also comes from using a "job platform" so that it fills a larger need, which can bring still wider responsibility and more power. The position and title—the "platform"—that McGeorge Bundy occupied in the Kennedy Administration existed in Eisenhower's day, but it was Bundy who made it powerful. Power comes from expertise, from representing a particular constituency, whether within or outside the government, from institutional backing, and from statutory or designated authority and responsibility. The mere title of the secretary of state gives a man authority, in addition to what he acquires through statute and custom.

The richness of the sources of power over the making of foreign policy goes back to the nature of the political process of conflict and consensus building by which policy is made. Within the government and outside it, to repeat, there are different constituencies with a stake in the outcome. The State Department may have jurisdiction over the general problem, for example, while the Pentagon must implement one aspect of it and the Agency for International Development another. Even if the President's prestige and position are not involved, his approval may be a legal or a political necessity. This may be true of Congress also. If so, the outside constituencies are likely to be drawn in—interest groups, newspapermen, academic commentators, and the still wider constituency of the particular attentive public.

In a major problem of foreign affairs, as we have said, the advocate of a particular policy, even if there is neither a rival advocate nor a rival policy, must build a consensus to support his policy in the different constituencies within the government and frequently outside as well. He needs the active cooperation and support of some, the formal or informal approval of others, and at least the acquiescence of still others. He may prevail over the active opposition of one or another constituency, but rarely if it is from within the government and the enterprise is large, for even passive opposition can bring a large and complicated enterprise to failure, not by sabotage, but simply by lack of enthusiasm. When there are rival advocates or rival policies, on the other hand, there is not only debate before the different constituencies, but competition for their support. Alliances are formed, and all the techniques of consensus building appear—persuasion, accommodation, and bargaining.

Over some of this at certain times the President may merely preside, if it is a matter of slight interest to him and has little impact on his position. But if *he* is an advocate or if the outcome affects *his* position and power, then the President, too, must engage in the politics of policy making. In the field of foreign affairs, the President's power is immense. His is the monopoly in dealing with other states. But he, too, must build a consensus for his policy if it is to succeed. He must bring along enough of the different factions in Congress to forestall revolt, and he must contend for the support of wider constituencies, the press, interest groups, and attentive publics. Even within the Executive branch itself, his policy will not succeed merely at his command, and he must build cooperation and support, obtain approval from some, acquiescence from others, and enthusiasm from enough to carry it to completion. This is the truth that Vice President Dawes was alluding to when he said that Cabinet ministers are a President's natural enemies. It is the truth that so amused President Truman when he said that Eisenhower would find that the Presidency was not "a bit like the Army." It is the truth that President Kennedy had in mind when he joked about the "inner club." It is the "half-observed realities," as Neustadt says, underneath our images of "Presidents-in-boots, astride decisions"—the realities of "Presidents-in-sneakers, stirrups in hand, trying to induce particular department heads, or congressmen, or senators to climb aboard."

A "POWER ELITE"?

One final question to be examined here is the recurring charge that policy in the United States, both domestic and foreign, is determined by a "power elite" or "establishment." The most famous and most often quoted of these charges are those of C. Wright Mills.[8] Mills argues that power in the United States is monopolized by three elites—military, economic, and political. "The power to make decisions of national and international consequence is now so clearly seated in political, military, and economic institutions that other areas of society seem off to the side and, on occasion, readily subordinated to these." Each of these big three, Mills asserts, has become increasingly interlocked with the others—that is, the economy has become a "war economy," dependent on the military; the military in turn depends upon industry; and both are the principal support of the political elite.

The result, Mills argues, has been the development of one overall power elite whose parts act together for their mutual interest that, in effect, conspires. "For as each of these domains has coincided with the others, as decisions in each have become broader, the leading men of each—the high

[8] The following is drawn from Mills's article, "The Structure of Power in American Society," *British Journal of Sociology* 9 (March 1958), where his argument is more succinctly stated than in his book.

military, the corporation executives, the political directorate
—have tended to come together to form the power elite of
America."

Mills stops short of asserting that all this has come about
as a result of a deliberate plot.

To say that these higher circles are increasingly coordinated, that
this is *one* basis of their unity, and that at times—as during open
war—such coordination is quite wilful, is not to say that the coordination is total or continuous, or even that it is very surefooted.
Much less is it to say that the power elite has emerged as the realization of a plot.

Even so, Mills asserts that the power elite is so unified that
the result is the same as if there had been a plot. This unity,
he argues, comes from several sources. One is social background.

To understand the unity of this power elite, we must pay attention
to the psychology of its several members in their respective milieux.
In so far as the power elite is composed of men of similar origin
and education, of similar career and style of life, their unity may be
said to rest upon the fact that they are of similar social type, and
to lead to the fact of their easy intermingling.

Another is the "interchangeability of positions," by which
Mills apparently means the fact that retired military men take
jobs in industry and so on. Still another is the common self-
interest of the three elites—"the development of a permanent-
war establishment, alongside a privately incorporated economy,
inside a virtual political vacuum."

Mills's overall vision of American society and basic conclusion is expressed in a single paragraph:

The top of modern American society is increasingly unified, and
often seems wilfully coordinated: at the top there has emerged
an elite whose power probably exceeds that of any small group
of men in world history. The middle levels are often a drifting set
of stalemated forces: the middle does not link the bottom with
the top. The bottom of this society is politically fragmented, and

even as a passive fact, increasingly powerless: at the bottom there is emerging a mass society.

Mills has been heavily criticized for his cavalier disregard of scientific method, rigor, and objectivity and for what amounts to deliberate disregard for facts. Talcott Parsons, the eminent sociologist, for example, points out that "Mills' close identification of the very rich (i.e., the holders of 'great fortunes') with the 'corporate rich' (the primary holders of executive power in business organizations) as a single class" cannot be accepted in any useful sense. "It is a notorious fact," Parsons goes on to say,

that the very large enterprise still under family control through property holdings is much more the exception than the rule. Instead, the control has passed—by no means fully, but for the most part—to professional career executives, who have not reached their positions through the exercise of property rights but through some sort of process of appointment and promotion.

Another ground for criticism is Mills's assertion that the power elite stem from similar social origins, while the examples he himself uses show a very wide diversity. One general mentioned by Mills, for example, is actually the adopted son of an Irish coal miner. Even the five Presidents since World War II illustrate a social diversity that is difficult to reconcile with Mills's assertion. Truman was the son of a middle western farmer. Eisenhower also came from the Middle West, but from a small-town background rather than farming. Neither had wealth. Kennedy was the son of a man who was very, very rich, but whose family was immigrant Irish and never fully accepted in aristocratic Boston. Johnson was the son of a Texas rancher, whose ranch was in the impoverished piedmont rather than the rich cattle lands. Nixon, finally, was the son of a grocery store owner in a small town in California. The only one of these who fits Mills's description is Kennedy, and even he lacked the social connections implied in some of Mills's assertions. To find a President who had the social connections as well as wealth, one would have to go back to Franklin D. Roosevelt, who came from an aristocratic New York family with old Dutch antecedents.

The criteria for proving the existence of a "power elite"

C. Wright Mills can be dismissed as little more than a pamphleteer, but the question of whether or not there is a "power elite" does deserve serious scholarly attention. Robert A. Dahl, partly in criticism of Mills and others like him, laid down the requirements necessary to demonstrate the existence of a power elite. First of all Dahl argues, "quasi-metaphysical theory made up of what might be called an infinite regress of explanations" must be ruled out. The following would be an example of an infinite regress of explanation: If it turns out that the overt leaders of a community are not a ruling elite, the theory can be saved by arguing that behind the overt there is a set of covert leaders. If the evidence shows that this covert group does not constitute a ruling elite, the theory again be saved by arguing that behind the first covert group there is another, and so on to infinity. Obviously, Dahl argues, a theory that cannot be tested by empirical evidence is not a scientific theory.

Dahl then rejects a number of "bad tests." One of these is confusing a ruling elite with a group that has a very high *potential for control*. Mills's "bureaucratic triumvirate" certainly has such a potential. The three military services, for example, have the brute strength and power to take over the country and establish a military dictatorship, if they all agreed on such a course. The evidence, on the contrary, is that they would find such a course abhorrent. A *potential* for control is not the same thing as actual control, or even significant influence. "The actual *political effectiveness* of a group," Dahl writes, "is a function of its potential for control *and* its potential for unity. Thus a group with a relatively low potential for control but a high potential for unity may be more politically effective than a group with a high potential for control but a low potential for unity."

The second improper test is to confuse a ruling elite with a group of individuals who have more influence than others. Obviously the President, the Secretary of State, and the Secretary of Defense have more influence over foreign policy than the rest of us, but that does not make a ruling elite.

The third improper test is "to generalize from a single scope of influence." Bankers, for example, have more influence than the rest of us on fiscal policy. Oil men have more influence on oil policy. Grange officials have more influence on agricultural policy. This is natural in the working of attentive publics, congressional constituencies, and so on as described in this book. Before it can be concluded that any one of these three is part of a ruling elite, it must be shown that it also has more influence than the rest of us on the full range of policy. If bankers and oil men are part of a ruling elite, they must be shown to have more influence over, say, agricultural policy than grange officials.

Dahl's conclusion is that the hypothesis of the existence of a ruling elite can be strictly tested only if:

1. The hypothetical ruling elite is a well-defined group.
2. There is a fair sample of cases involving key political decisions in which the preferences of the hypothetical ruling elite run counter to those of any other likely group that might be suggested.
3. In such cases, the preferences of the elite regularly prevail.

As the evidence in this book suggests, if this threefold test is used, the United States has no ruling elite in any meaningful sense. A wide variety of people are involved in the making of United States foreign policy—the President, the members of the Cabinet, other members of an administration, civilian and military officials in all the great departments and agencies, ambassadors and their staffs overseas, members of the Congress, the press, members of the attentive publics, interest groups, specialists and experts in universities and research organizations, and, on occasion, the mass public. This is too wide a spectrum to constitute a ruling elite, and even those who are most intimately involved, the President, congressmen, and other high officials, do not come from any one class or social grouping.

Again from the evidence in this book, there is certainly little unity even within the group of people most intimately concerned. On every major issue of foreign policy there has been disagreement, and usually the differences have cut across institutional lines. There have been military "doves," for example, as well as military "hawks."

When faced with this evidence, some proponents of the ruling elite theory will concede that government officials, members of Congress, and so on do not come from a particular social class and will also concede that there is no evidence of any ruling elite, overt or covert, giving them orders (i.e., no evidence that the big corporations, for example, have any direct voice on, say, Vietnam policy). But, they argue, all these officials share an American "capitalist-imperialist" outlook, and they make their foreign policy decisions in the interests of the big corporations (or Mills's military-economic-political power elite) without being told. Now this is very close to one of the "quasi-metaphysical" theories that Dahl describes, but it also cannot be denied that the people who make United States foreign policy are Americans and that Americans do share certain attitudes. The trouble is that the attitudes which foreign observers agree that Americans share are too general to be a guide to specific foreign policy decisions. Most foreign observers agree, for example, that Americans are pragmatic, activist, and egalitarian, but none of these qualities necessarily suggests that American foreign policy in the Middle East, for example, will be conducted to serve the interest of the oil companies.

In addition the general assertion that the people involved in making United States foreign policy have an ingrained "capitalist-imperialist" outlook that leads them to act in the interest of the big corporations ignores a number of deeply ingrained attitudes that are hostile to those interests. There is a populist tradition in America, strongly held by a number of powerful congressmen, for example, that regards the big corporations and the eastern seaboard financial interests as greater enemies than either communism or fascism. There is an isolationist sentiment that runs equally strong.

The assertion that United States foreign policy is conducted to serve the interests of the big corporations also ignores United States foreign policy. It is obvious to even the most casual observer, for example, that United States foreign policy in the Middle East, where oil reigns supreme, has been more responsive to the pressures from the American Jewish community and their natural desire to support Israel than it has to American oil interests.

H. L. Hunt and the National Rifle Association

The proponents of a ruling elite theory believe that the evil in America is a result of the concentration of power in its government and society, but in fact the opposite is more nearly the case. Consider two examples, H. L. Hunt and the National Rifle Association. H. L. Hunt, the Texas oil multimillionaire, is purported to be the richest man in the United States, if not the entire world. He is, clearly, an outstanding candidate for a high place in C. Wright Mills's ruling elite. His views on social questions, his policy preferences, can best be described as right-wing extremist. He is opposed to civil rights, to social security, to medicare, and so on. He has spent a great deal of money to further his policy preferences, but he has in general failed. The members of the National Rifle Association, on the other hand, in general do not qualify for membership in Mills's ruling elite. They tend to be lower middle class, from rural and small-town backgrounds. But on one issue, gun control legislation, they have prevailed against all comers. For over thirty years, public opinion polls have shown that more than 60 percent of Americans favor gun control legislation. In addition a formidable array of people that should be part of the ruling elite have worked hard to get an effective gun control law—including Nelson A. Rockefeller, Governor of New York, and, for obvious reasons, Edward M. Kennedy, Senator from Massachusetts. But the NRA, with a

membership of 825,000—fewer than a million—has prevailed. One half of 1 percent has blocked 60 percent. In a
society in which power is diffused, a minority that feels in-
tensely can often have its will over a majority that feels dif-
ferently but not so strongly.

The truth is that many of the evils in American society—the
long oppression of the blacks, the decline of the cities, water
and air pollution, and so on—stem not from the concentration of power, but at least in part from its diffusion. The very
profusion of so many centers of power makes building the
kind of consensus necessary for positive measures a formidable task.

NINE
IMPROVING THE POLICY MACHINERY: ORGANIZATION AND REORGANIZATION

HOW can United States foreign policy be improved? Whenever the question comes up, attention turns first to the question of organization and how the State Department, the National Security Council, or the White House might be reorganized. The experience with reorganization, however, has not always been good.

Dean Acheson used to tell a story about Chief Justice Taft relating a conversation he had just had with an eminent man about the "machinery" of government. "And you know," Taft said with wonder in his voice, "he really does believe it *is* machinery."

Of one thing we can be sure: it is not machinery. There was a day when political scientists spent a great deal of their time on organization charts, moving boxes here and there in accordance with principles based on a distinction between administration and management, on the one hand, and policy and politics, on the other. They do no longer.

Arguments about organization can arouse high passion. This is partly because organizational struggles are struggles for personal power and position. The outcome of the battle can be a more or less formal confirmation of who ended up with power over what kind of policy. Not everyone, however, strives for power. Secretary Rusk noted the phenomenon in the following words:

The processes of government have sometimes been described as a struggle for power among those holding public office. I am convinced that this is true only in a certain formal and bureaucratic sense, having to do with appropriations, job descriptions, trappings of prestige, water bottles and things of that sort. There is another struggle of far more consequence, the effort to diffuse or avoid responsibility. Power gravitates to those who are willing to make decisions and live with the results, simply because there are so many who readily yield to the intrepid few who take their duties seriously.

Men who are concerned with the substance of policy will seek power in order to influence policy; men who are concerned only with the trappings and titles will seek not to acquire responsibility but to diffuse and evade it. Part of the organizational shuffling in Washington, in other words, is a scramble to get off target zero.

But the struggle over organization in Washington is also considerably more than an attempt either to acquire personal power or to evade it. Apart from very obvious efficiencies or inefficiencies, in so complicated a business as the making of national policy there is probably no good or bad organization except in terms of what one regards as good or bad policy.[1] By making it easier for some people to have access than others, by providing for the accumulation of one kind of information and not another, or by following procedures that let some problems rise to the top of the government's agenda before others—in all these ways some organizational arrangements facilitate certain kinds of policy and other organizational arrangements facilitate other kinds of policy. One example was when Theodore Roosevelt tried to establish conservation of natural resources as national policy in place of

[1] On this point see Warner R. Schilling, "The Politics of National Defense: Fiscal 1950," in Schilling, Hammond, and Snyder, *Strategy, Politics and Defense Budgets* (1962), pp. 16–17.

the older, homesteading policy of creating incentives for clearing the forests and peopling the land. The old organizational arrangements provided easy channels for lumbering and other exploitative interests to express their preferences and almost none for conservationist interests to express theirs. There were almost no mechanisms for gathering the kind of information that would permit governmental decisions to conserve rather than exploit. The result was that President Roosevelt could not really change from a policy of encouraging homesteading to a policy of encouraging conservation until he changed the organization dealing with the problem.

So whether one thinks a certain organizational arrangement is "good" or "bad" depends on what one thinks of the kind of policy it facilitates. This, too, has its repercussions. We have said that policy making is essentially a political process, by which the multiplicity of goals and values in a free and diverse society are reconciled and the debate over means and ends is distilled into a politically viable consensus on a workable policy. But if some organizational arrangements facilitate certain kinds of policy and other arrangements facilitate other kinds, then organization is also politics in still another guise— which accounts for the passion that men so often bring to procedural and organizational matters.

THE ROOSEVELT ERA

The contemporary governmental machinery for national security policy began in the Roosevelt Administration. In 1937 the President's Committee on Administration Management, headed by Louis Brownlow, recommended setting up what Richard E. Neustadt has called a "President's Department." The central recommendation was to put the Bureau of the Budget directly under the President, as an integral part of the "Executive Office" of the President. It was the first of what has become a considerable number of organizations that are part of the institution of the Presidency, but not actually part of the President's personal staff.

The Brownlow report also provided the President with additional personal staff, administrative assistants, whom the President could use either as roving generalists or on fixed assignment, such as liason work with the Congress.

This arrangement gave Franklin D. Roosevelt the flexibility he wanted, for he had a free and easy style that plucked advice and information from every conceivable and even casual source, and he also built into the relationship between departments, Cabinet officers, and even his personal staff a competition that he also used to gain flexibility. Out of the competition and glorious disorder, he could develop policy alternatives, test them on a wide variety of people, and ensure that it was he and not someone else who made the choices at his timing.

THE NATIONAL SECURITY COUNCIL

The next major organizational development came immediately after World War II with the National Security Act of 1947 which set up the National Security Council, as well as created a separate air force and the Central Intelligence Agency. The NSC setup came out of studies in the Pentagon, sponsored mainly by James V. Forrestal, Secretary of the Navy and later the first Secretary of Defense. It was, in truth, a reaction to Roosevelt's free and easy style, which often left one or another department, agency, or high official out of what he felt he should legitimately be in. The NSC setup was designed to make sure that all the major departments, and especially the Department of Defense, had a regular voice. It tried to pin down future Presidents in a way that Roosevelt would never permit himself to be pinned down, and the NSC was as much a reaction to Roosevelt, the man, and his way of operating as the amendment limiting Presidents to two terms. The NSC, in fact, has been called "Forrestal's Revenge" in what is only half a jest,[2] for Forrestal was trying to ensure a Defense

[2] Richard E. Neustadt, "Approaches to Staffing the Presidency: Notes on FDR and JFK," *American Political Science Review* (December 1963).

Department voice in foreign policy to make sure that our strength was always consistent with our commitments.

THE EISENHOWER ADMINISTRATION

President Eisenhower, of course, had grown up with military administrative procedures, and although he had extensive experience with high policy, it was not of a kind to make him doubt the soundness of military procedures. His experience with high policy had been in wartime. It certainly included a significant share of international political problems, beginning with Admiral Darlan in North Africa. But in time of war the overall goal of winning a victory mutes the raw politics of reconciling a multiplicity of competing goals and hostile interests that is the stuff of day-by-day affairs. President Eisenhower, accordingly, took the set of institutions he had inherited and made them into something very similar to the formalized, hierarchical military procedures with which he was so familiar.

To the basic NSC structure, Eisenhower added a Planning Board and an Operations Coordinating Board. Thus policy in the Eisenhower Administration was made by a hierarchy of interdepartmental committees, proceding step by step up the ladder until it arrived at the NSC itself, which met weekly with the President as Chairman. Then, after a formal decision, the Operations Coordinating Board took over with monthly, quarterly, and annual reviews, including mountains of follow-up memoranda to ensure that each department and agency carried out the approved policy.[3]

There were indications that President Eisenhower and other top members of his Administration were considering going even farther along these lines; proposals kept circulating in Washington for creating a second vice president, to be in charge of foreign affairs, for strengthening the NSC, or for

[3] For a description of the workings of the NSC structure during the Eisenhower Administration, see Robert Cutler, "The Development of the National Security Council," *Foreign Affairs*, April 1956.

increasing the power of the special assistant to the President for National Security Affairs (a post held in the Eisenhower Administration by Robert Cutler and Gordon Grey, in the Kennedy Administration by McGeorge Bundy, and in the Johnson Administration by Bundy first and then Walt W. Rostow).

The idea behind the Eisenhower way of organizing the government was that the top men should save their strength and wisdom for what the officials lower down were unable to decide, and the pressure was toward reconciling differences at as low a level in the hierarchy as possible so as to give the top leadership an agreed "best" solution. The assumption behind this notion was that an administration is a "team"— one of President Eisenhower's favorite words—rather like an idealized British cabinet that had common interests and ideology.

In a sense the assumption was correct, for such an organizational arrangement did tend to produce the kind of basically conservative policies that the dominant elements of the Eisenhower Administration desired. It naturally discouraged new and innovating policies by its pressure for agreement on a "best" solution, which usually resulted in agreement on the lowest common denominator of competing departmental interests and concerns. In foreign policy, particularly, its effect was to emphasize policies supporting the status quo, with a high value on "stability" in individual countries and regions.

The Democrats attack

Long before the end of the Eisenhower Administration, the Democrats began to attack the Republicans' organizational ideas and to develop some of their own. Dean Acheson, as the last Democratic Secretary of State, summed up their views in an article entitled "Thoughts about Thought in High Places."[4] When Dulles had taken over Acheson's post as Secretary, he said that he intended to organize the Department of

[4] Dean Acheson, "Thoughts about Thought in High Places," New York Times Magazine, October 11, 1959.

State so that he would have time to think. Ridiculing the idea that in policy making thought could be so divorced from action, Acheson predicted that the result would always be as it turned out with the Eisenhower NSC structure—to cut the chief off from his principal officers and interpose a "coordinating staff" between them and the chief. "The result," Acheson wrote, "will be that he will have to see just as many people, but they will be the wrong people."

As for the idea that the purpose of good organizations is to see that as many problems as possible are decided as low in the hierarchy as possible—in the form of "agreed" papers—Acheson argued the exact opposite. The true purpose of good organization, he maintained, was to furnish, where there was any doubt at all about the wise course, not agreed papers, but "disagreed" papers. The need, Acheson felt, was for papers in which the issues are laid out and the alternatives argued as fully and persuasively as the different advocates knew how. The Democrats' position, in sum, was that trying to make a decision-making body out of the NSC had been a failure, for there are differing interests in the different departments, and it is the true job of these departments to defend these interests as best they can. To ask these same people to decide on the "best" solution is to ask them to find the lowest common denominator, to invite them to reconcile differences by papering them over with a policy so general as neither to serve nor damage the interests of the competing participants.

The academic community

The academic community also weighed in against the Eisenhower Administration's reliance on the NSC structure and ridiculed the suggestions for strengthening it further and for creating "czars" such as a vice president for foreign affairs.[5]

[5] A representative sample would include the following: Hans Morganthau, "Can We Entrust Defense to a Committee?" *New York Times Magazine,* June 7, 1959; Don K. Price, ed., for the American Assembly, *The Secretary of State,* (1960); George F. Kennan, "America's Administrative Response to Its World Problems," *Daedalus* 87 (Spring 1958); Henry A. Kissinger, "The Policy Maker and the Intellectual," *Reporter,* March 5, 1959; W. W.

The literature is large, but one article, which was a group effort, will serve as an example of the current of academic thought at the time.[6] The conclusion reached by the group was that any attempt to strengthen the NSC would erect more obstacles than it would remove. Measures like creating a vice president for foreign affairs, the group felt, would put still another layer between the President and the problems which only he could decide, and add still more to the pressures for agreed positions at the cost of clarity and concreteness. No good, they were convinced, could come of creating a rival of the secretary of state in the area of his own responsibility, for policy making is not the kind of work that is necessarily facilitated by creating a czar. The expediter with extraordinary powers may often be the answer to a production problem or to getting a crash program on the road, but producing policy is different from producing hardware and does not yield to the same expedients. The NSC is a device by which the different departments concerned with national security can meet, discuss their problems and differences, reconcile unimportant disagreements, and when it comes to major disagreements at least poke holes in one anothers' arguments— all in the presence of and for the benefit of the President. Its function, the group argued, is that of a forum for debate and through debate that of a channel for information, but nothing more.

The conclusion reached by the group was that any attempt to make the NSC into something more than this—into a true decision-making body similar, for example, to the Cabinet in the British parliamentary system—would be frustrated. In the first place, the President, unlike the British Prime Minister, does not need the direct support of his Cabinet secre-

Rostow, "The Fallacy of the Fertile Gondolas," *Harvard Alumni Bulletin,* May 25, 1957; Paul H. Nitze, "Organization for National Policy Planning in the United States," paper presented to the American Political Science Association, September 1959.
[6] Roger Hilsman, ed., "Planning for National Security: A Proposal," *Bulletin of the Atomic Scientists* (March 1960).

taries and fellow party members in the legislature to continue in office, and Cabinet secretaries in the United States do not represent segments of political power in quite the same way as ministers do in Britain. In the second place, the argument continued, for many policies a wider consent seems to be needed than can be represented in a body like the NSC, and such a body is hardly suitable for making the bilateral arrangements that may be necessary in developing that wider consent, for bargaining, or for the weighing and balancing of power that a political process entails. The question, the group concluded, was not so much one of organization, but of policy and purpose; the existing arrangements could be made to produce "good" policy or "bad" policy, depending on who used them, for what purpose, and how.

Congress and the Jackson Subcommittee

Perhaps the most important work of all on organizational problems in this period was done in Congress, by the Jackson Subcommittee. It was an outstanding example of a creative, responsible, and constructive use of the congressional power to investigate, conduct studies, and explore.

Senator Henry M. Jackson's Subcommittee on National Policy Machinery of the Committee on Government Operations, to give its official title, began work in July, 1959 with a first-rate staff drawn from the universities and from among former officials of the State Department. Hearings were conducted with men like Robert A. Lovett, Nelson Rockefeller, Admiral Arthur W. Radford, General Maxwell D. Taylor, and the then Secretaries of State, Defense, and Treasury. The results were a series of reports that began to come out in the fall of 1960 and early spring of 1961, perfectly timed to influence the organizational struggles of the new Administration under John F. Kennedy.

The subcommittee's conclusions were blunt and to the point. Any idea of radical additions to the existing policy machinery or of "super-cabinet officers and super staffs" was rejected. "Our best hope," the final report read, "lies in making our traditional policy machinery work better—not in trading it in for some new model." The subcommittee harshly criticized the heavy undergrowth of interdepartmental committees clustered around the NSC and particularly the cumbersome Operations Coordinating Board. "The case for abolishing the OCB," said the subcommittee's report on NSC structure, "is strong." But the major theme was that no task was more urgent than improving the effectiveness of the Department of State. The subcommittee pushed hard for better people down the line, for "take charge" men, particularly at the assistant secretary level, but it pushed even harder for the idea that the State Department should *lead*. "In our system," the final report read, "there can be no satisfactory substitute for a Secretary of State willing and able to exercise his leadership across the full range of national security matters. . . ."

THE KENNEDY ADMINISTRATION

If the organizational arrangements of the Eisenhower Administration produced status quo policies and discouraged innovation, the Kennedy Administration wanted something different. The Kennedy Administration was activist in foreign policy, oriented to the emerging peoples and new nationalisms, and determined to attempt to shape events. If the object was to produce policies for these purposes, it seemed to make sense to put power in the hands of those whose responsibilities would make them politically oriented and concerned with the whole of foreign problems—the Department of State.

In any case President Kennedy seemed to agree with this general approach, and he moved rapidly to clear the organizational decks. Within a month of taking office, he abolished the Operations Coordinating Board and relegated the Planning Board to what became a luncheon discussion group. In his statement announcing the action, the President said that his Administration planned to do the Board's work in other ways. "First," he said, "we will center responsibility for much of the Board's work in the Secretary of State. He expects to rely particularly on the Assistant Secretaries in charge of regional bureaus, and they in turn will consult closely with other departments and agencies. This will be our ordinary rule for continuing coordination of our work in relation to a country or area." Something over forty-five interdepartmental committees died with the OCB, and the White House killed another thirty or forty in the next few weeks. Instead of regular weekly meetings, the NSC met only for special problems, and there were only sixteen such occasions in the first six months. Thus the general thrust was to give responsibility for leadership to the Department of State.

In a letter to Senator Jackson, whose subcommittee was following up its earlier work, McGeorge Bundy summed up the changes the new Administration had made in the NSC structure, and again the theme was that responsibility was being given to the Department of State. Recalling that Robert Cutler, the principal Eisenhower aide in the NSC, had praised the flexibility of the NSC structure and had stressed that "each President may use the Council as he finds most suitable at a given time," Bundy said that three specific changes had occurred in the Kennedy Administration. The first was that the NSC met less often than in the Eisenhower Administration, only sixteen times in the first six months, as already mentioned. Bundy went on to describe smaller, less formal meetings in which many of the same people were present; these meetings developed into what was called the "Executive Committee" at the time of the Cuban missile crisis a year later.

Bundy regarded the abolition of the Operations Coordinating Board as the second major development. Arguing that this was not in any sense a downgrading of the tasks of coordination and follow-up but a move to eliminate an instrument that did not match the style of the new Administration, Bundy went on to say that the OCB was a committee in which no member had authority over any other and that its work could be better done in other ways. "The most important of these other ways," Bundy wrote, "is an increased reliance on the leadership of the Department of State."

The third change Bundy described was the new Administration's action to rub out the distinction between planning and operations in the work of the White House staff. Under Kennedy this staff was smaller than it was under the previous Administration, and, according to Bundy, more closely knit. "Their job," he wrote,

is to help the President, not to supersede or supplement any of the high officials who hold the line responsibilities in the executive departments and agencies. . . . Heavy responsibilities for operation, for coordination, and for diplomatic relations can be and are delegated to the Department of State. Full use of all the powers of leadership can be and is expected in other departments and agencies. There remains a crushing burden of responsibility, and of sheer work, on the President himself; there remains also the steady flow of questions, of ideas, of executive energy which a strong President will give off like sparks. If his Cabinet officers are to be free to do their own work, the President's work must be done— to the extent that he cannot do it himself—by staff officers under his direct oversight.

The final confirmation that Kennedy had decided to make the Department of State and its Secretary, Dean Rusk, the key element in the national security policy-making machinery came in a speech to the policy officers of the department by the Secretary of State, a speech made at the instigation of the President. Describing a "world of change," the Secretary called upon the officers of the Department to assume the "leadership of change," to reduce the "infant mortality rate of ideas," to assume responsibility not only for the formulation but the active coordination of policy. The climax of the speech came in the paragraph quoted at the beginning of this chapter—the ringing words in which the Secretary declared that power gravitates to those who are willing to make decisions and called upon the officers of the Department of State to be among those "intrepid few." The department, he said, "is entering, I think, something of a new phase in its existence. We are expected to take charge."

Practice versus theory

Within a matter of weeks, however, it became clear that the President's expectations about the State Department were doomed to disappointment. Crises arose, but rather than "taking charge," the State Department seemed ill-prepared and occasionally befuddled. The Secretary of State himself seemed to want to hold back, and everyone else began to hold back too. To force action the President began to appoint interdepartmental task forces, and as the State Department seemed to be increasingly reluctant to assume the leadership role, he showed his irritation by giving the chairmanship of two important task forces to Defense Department officials rather than State Department officials. The chairmanship of the Berlin task force went to the Assistant Secretary of Defense for International Security Affairs, Paul H. Nitze, and that of the Vietnam Task Force to the Deputy Secretary of Defense, Roswell Gilpatric.

The climax of the President's dissatisfaction with the State Department's failure to respond to his decision to give it the major role of leadership came with the Bay of Pigs fiasco. Although the President himself assumed full responsibility for the decisions leading to the disaster, it was clear to everyone concerned that both the CIA and the State Department bore a large share of the blame. The fault of the CIA had been in becoming so emotionally involved in one of their secret schemes as to become blind to its faults and dangers. The fault of the State Department and its Secretary was, first, in refusing to take a strong stand, in not insisting that the veil of secrecy imposed by the CIA be lifted at least enough to permit State Department experts on Cuba to be consulted. But the greater fault was the failure of both the Secretary and the department to make the case for political considerations that should have been made. It was an abdication of the role of leadership that the President had assigned.

The Kennedy compromise

President Kennedy took several weeks to decide what he would do. His solution was to retain Rusk as Secretary of State, but to replace a substantial number of the people directly under him—the Undersecretary and several of the Assistant Secretaries—with men who had a close personal relationship with the President himself. He then proceeded to exercise direct supervision of foreign affairs himself.

This is not to say that President Kennedy had set out to be his own Secretary of State, as has sometimes been alleged, or that he had conducted his original search for a man to be secretary with that in mind. He was looking for the most experienced and able man he could find—without, of course, taking on someone with serious political liabilities—and on balance Dean Rusk most closely filled the bill of any of the men available.[7]

It is one of the drawbacks of a Presidential-congressional system of government that so few men can acquire the combination of experience in both foreign affairs and domestic politics needed by a secretary of state and that, consequently, a President has so few choices. President Kennedy needed a man, first of all, who had competency and stature in the field of foreign affairs. If that man also had political experience and was himself a public figure who could bring public support without political liability, so much the better. Lincoln found such a man in Seward once Seward stopped thinking that it was he who really should have been in the White House and began to be the President's man. President Harrison tried with James G. Blaine, the Mr. Republican of his day, but Blaine never really stepped down to be the President's man. Truman tried and failed for the same reason with James F. Byrnes, who always felt that Truman

[7] See my *To Move a Nation*, pp. 52–53, for a fuller treatment of this point.

had gotten the Vice Presidential nomination that he, Byrnes, had really deserved. Truman finally found Dean Acheson who had some public stature and was well known at least to the makers of public opinion, the press, and the Congress, if not to the public at large. Acheson had also had very considerable experience in foreign affairs. Eisenhower had found almost exactly the same combination in John Foster Dulles, although he was perhaps even better known to the public, since there had been much speculation four years earlier that he would be Dewey's choice for Secretary if Dewey were elected in 1948. Each of these Presidents as a practical political matter never had more than half a dozen men to choose from.

The names mentioned for secretary of state at the time President Kennedy was choosing his cabinet were Adlai Stevenson, the Democratic candidate for President in 1952 and 1956; J. William Fulbright, Senator from Arkansas and Chairman of the Senate Foreign Relations Committee; Chester Bowles, former Governor of Connecticut, Ambassador to India, and head of OPA; W. Averell Harriman, former Governor of New York, Ambassador to Moscow and London, and head of the Marshall Plan; and Robert A. Lovett, who had served both as Under Secretary of State and as Secretary of Defense in former administrations. All these men brought public stature as well as competency and experience in foreign affairs, but all were disqualified for one reason or another. Stevenson might be just as hard to manage for a younger President with a narrow election victory as Blaine or Byrnes had been, and the opposition in Congress to his liberal views and the reputation he had acquired for indecisiveness might balance off the considerable public support he brought to the job. Harriman was felt to be too old— wrongly it turned out if one is to judge by his subsequent long years of service. Bowles was judged too liberal to get along well with Congress. And the fact that Fulbright was a southerner would make it difficult for him to carry out United States foreign policy in Asia and Africa. President Kennedy offered Lovett the job, but his health was such that he could not accept it. Thus in the end the President chose Dean Rusk —who had been Assistant Secretary of State for Far Eastern Affairs, in the Truman Administration, and Assistant Secretary for International Organization Affairs as well as President of the Rockefeller Foundation in the meantime—as the most experienced and highly recommended man among a second group of those who had neither the stature nor were so well known as the front runners.

In justifying his decision to retain Rusk and take more of the direction of foreign affairs himself, President Kennedy told people who were close to him that organizations were made up of people, and that a President had to adjust to a set of personalities just as they had to adjust to him.

The White House and the Defense Department

Kennedy's adjustment to the Defense Department was rather straightforward. He had very well-developed ideas about strategic matters, fully formed in the great national debate on "massive retaliation," the "missile gap," and so on that took place over the six years from 1954 to 1960. He believed in balanced forces and the capacity for "flexible response." In Robert McNamara he found a Secretary of Defense who shared his views, who had the imagination to push those views even farther down the line of their logical development, and who had the will for strong leadership. "I see my position here as being that of a leader, not a judge," McNamara once said. "I'm here to originate and stimulate new ideas and programs, not just to referee arguments and harmonize interests. Using deliberate analysis to force alternative programs to the surface, and then making explicit choices among them is fundamental."[8]

Kennedy could comfortably let McNamara be Secretary of Defense while he remained as President—giving broad policy direction and taking care through a variety of means, including an active White House staff, that he was made aware of

[8] W. W. Kaufmann, *The McNamara Strategy* (1964), p. 171.

the policy issues and alternatives down the line in the Defense Department in time for him to intervene effectively when and if he chose. The only problem that required exceptional care was that McNamara's boundless energy and formidable ability sometimes tempted him to use whatever military component there was in a political problem as a beachhead. Occasionally he extended the beachhead until he came very near to dominating the whole affair—for example, relations with Europe at the time of the Berlin crisis, the political situation in Saigon in a later day, or relations with India following the 1962 frontier war with China. Such vigorous excursions into foreign political affairs by those charged with military responsibilities is not necessarily bad—just as equally vigorous excursions by the State Department into military and strategic matters might at times be good—so long as there are strong and knowledgeable men in the one department defending politcal considerations and equally strong and knowledgeable men defending military considerations in the other. But it does require an alert President in constant supervision.

It was McGeorge Bundy's job to police this area where political and military considerations overlap and to keep the Administration together. In the Kennedy Administration, Bundy avoided being an advocate of policy, although he frequently was called upon to act as judge and did so, as on occasion did everyone who attended meetings at the White House. His role in the period leading up to a decision was to be the midwife of policy, to anticipate problems coming up, to see that the staff work was fully done, that all departments, agencies, and segments of the Administration that had a legitimate concern had a full opportunity to present their views, and that no aspect of the problem itself was neglected. Then, after the decision, his responsibility was to follow through, to see that each department did its part in implementing the policy, but especially to see that the President's interests were protected.

Thus to some extent, it was Bundy and the White House staff who performed the function of ensuring that issues were exposed, that policy alternatives were developed and not masked over, and that the President had the opportunity to make choices, and at his timing. Like Roosevelt, Kennedy made sure to build a certain amount of competition into the relationships between departments.

Adjusting to the State Department

President Kennedy's adjustment to the State Department was more complicated than his adjustment to the Defense Department. This was partly because Dean Rusk's conception of his job as Secretary of State was more complicated than McNamara's conception of his job as Secretary of Defense.

Dean Acheson clearly would have agreed with the idea developed by the Jackson Subcommittee and the incoming Kennedy Administration that the secretary of state should be leader and advocate of policy, which would require him to manage the State Department itself, and at the same time the chief coordinator of those policies that cut across several departments in the area of foreign affairs, because of the preeminence of political considerations over the economic or military. Acheson also understood the implications of this view in terms of how exposed a secretary who tries to be advocate and leader can be to public and congressional attack. He once wrote that in Washington the President and the secretary of state were "working in an environment where some of the methods would have aroused the envy of the Borgias."[9] He also understood the other set of implications, what such a role requires *from* the secretary of state if he is to be the coordinator of policy and maintain the preeminence of the political over the economic and the military. When a foreign colleague once asked him to name the quality most required in an American secretary of state, he replied, "The killer instinct." And Acheson followed his own advice. When he was himself faced with a very ambitious secretary of defense who reached aggressively beyond the Pentagon for

[9] Dean Acheson, "The President and the Secretary of State," in the American Assembly's *The Secretary of State* (1960).

dominance over the whole spectrum of policy, he forced a showdown, and before it was over, true to his "killer instinct," his opponent, Louis Johnson, had been fired.

Rusk, on the other hand, seemed to feel that it was inappropriate for the secretary of state to do battle in the name of the department, even for the important cause of maintaining the preeminence of political considerations. Rather than doing battle in the name of the State Department, or even representing it, Rusk seemed to see himself as standing somewhat apart, more as a personal adviser to the President than as representing any particular point of view, even the political. He seemed to view the secretary not as the maker and advocate of policy, but, at the President's side, as a judge. Thus the President, in Rusk's view, should give leadership in terms of overall goals and objectives, in terms of grand policy. The assistant secretaries, concentrating on particular regions, should be the formulators and advocates of specific policies and the managers of the State Department. But the position of secretary of state he seemed to see as being above and apart from all this, permitting the incumbent to sit alongside the President in judgment precisely because he was free of the restraints and commitments of representing a department.

Not many people who know Washington would share Rusk's conception of the secretaryship, but it is logical and internally consistent, providing a meaningful and useful role around which a President can build an effective organizational arrangement. Like all organizational notions, it has both advantages and disadvantages.

The disadvantages are principally that when a secretary of state sits to one side as a judge, the political considerations must be upheld by the assistant secretaries. When they are faced with the secretary of defense, the joint chiefs of staff, and the director of the CIA, the contest is highly unequal. This is essentially what was behind the fiasco of the Bay of Pigs decision.

The only way this fault can be remedied is for the President to act as his own secretary of state, which is what happened in the Kennedy Administration after the Bay of Pigs and throughout the Johnson Administration. If a President acts as his own secretary, however, Rusk's conception of the secretary's role does have advantages. Rusk has been much criticized, but consistent with his conception of the secretaryship, he served both Kennedy and Johnson well. Paradoxically, the one major problem area in which Rusk seems to have abandoned his conception of the secretary as a judge and become a passionate advocate was the most tragic mistake of all—turning the struggle in Vietnam into an American war by the decision in 1965 to bomb North Vietnam and send American ground forces.

The advantage of Rusk's conception was that he was able to represent a point of view, corresponding closely with responsible, conservative opinion among congressmen, that was essential for both Presidents to consider. Patiently, and with calm dignity, he explained the complexities of the world and defended the President's policy, whatever it was, to the men on Capitol Hill. By his modesty and restraint he made easier the President's task of keeping the great departments and their sometimes imperious leaders working together toward a common goal.

So it was in both the Kennedy and Johnson Administrations. In defense matters both Presidents worked mainly with Secretary McNamara, relying on McNamara himself, on Bundy, and later on Walt W. Rostow as National Security Adviser in the White House to keep open the President's own options for choice. In the State Department both Presidents made full use of Rusk's talents as a judge, as adviser, and as representative on Capitol Hill; it is clear that they respected his judgment. But in both Administrations, it was the President himself who was, in McNamara's phrase, the "leader, not the judge" at the State Department, who was there "to originate and stimulate new ideas and programs, not just to referee arguments and harmonize interests." This task, as well as the task of coordinating and managing the whole range of security policy that the Kennedy Administration had intended to assign to the State Department was assumed in both the Kennedy and Johnson Administrations by the President himself.

THE NIXON ADMINISTRATION

Although still in its early years, the Nixon Administration has produced no new organizational arrangements. The President seems satisfied with the National Security Council setup, and uses it with a personal style that is perhaps more formal and hierarchical than that used by either Kennedy or Johnson.

As to the adjustment of personalities, Nixon has in Henry A. Kissinger, a strong and exceptionally well-informed and knowledgeable White House adviser on National Security Affairs. In Melvin Laird he also has a strong, knowledgeable, and able Secretary of Defense. The Secretary of State, William P. Rogers, seems to be less well informed and knowledgeable than either Kissinger or Laird. It is perhaps for this reason that Nixon seems to be acting like his own Secretary of State in certain problem areas, notably Vietnam. It also appears that on a number of other matters, particularly policy toward Africa, Rogers is behaving like a Secretary in the tradition of Acheson rather than Rusk.

TEN
IMPROVING THE
POLICY-MAKING PROCESS

FOREIGN policy is politics, and politics, in Max Weber's phrase, is a "slow boring of hard boards." There is probably no quick or easy way to make improvements. Certainly it seems clear from the experience of recent administrations, as we have seen, that tinkering with the organizational machinery does not hold much promise. At the end of the Eisenhower Administration, after the preceding experience under Roosevelt and Truman, there was a debate on "organizing for national security." The conclusion, to repeat, was that "super-staffs and super-secretaries" were no way to do this, and neither was "strengthening" the National Security Council or creating a "vice-president for foreign affairs." Certainly nothing happened in the Kennedy, Johnson, or Nixon Administrations that would alter that conclusion. In fact, the major recommendation that came out of the debate—that the prime voice and coordinating power should center in the Department of State—in practice only proved the validity of the conclusion that reorganizing was no solution. Merely assigning power to the State Department did not guarantee that the secretary and the department would use it.

All this, of course, does not mean that changes in organization do not affect policy. Organizational changes usually follow a shift in power as, for example, the changes in the way intelligence problems were handled in the State Department followed the CIA's loss of power in the aftermath of the Bay of Pigs. But changes in organization can in themselves bring about an increase or decrease of power and alter the weight that one set of considerations will have over another in policy deliberations. Whether the result is better or worse policy depends on one's point of view and on whose interests are being given additional weight. What is an "improvement" in this sense to one person may not be to another.

Some improvements that everyone would agree were improvements are undoubtedly possible in organizational structure. Ways might be found, for example, to make the communications process among participants in the making of policy quicker and easier. There might also be organizational changes that could bring more precision in assigning the flow of work, or in the effectiveness of applying the proper expertise at the proper stage. But these are not of fundamental importance and would result in only marginal improvement in the foreign policies that came out the other end.

PREDICTION AND KNOWLEDGE

Effective foreign policy depends on the capacity to predict events in the social affairs of men, and a better capacity to predict would mean better and more effective foreign policy. But more is required than simple factual information. Predicting the outcome of alternative policies requires knowledge in the sense of an ability to identify and weigh the different factors bearing on the particular situation and an understanding of the dynamism by which those different factors interact.[1] In the Middle Ages, for example, no one foresaw the Black Death or knew what to do about it after it came. Yet when

[1] For discussions of the role of facts and the role of theory, see Morris R. Cohen, *Reason and Nature* (1959) and my *Strategic Intelligence and National Decisions* (1956).

they learned that germs cause disease and the means by which germs are transmitted, men could not only treat individual cases of the plague, but could foresee that an increase in filth in the cities and the rats that live on it would create the conditions for an outbreak of the plague and indicate the measures needed to head it off.

There is no doubt that knowledge in this sense of the ability to make sound predictions is the crux of the matter. The debate over Vietnam policy in the Kennedy, Johnson, and Nixon Administrations, for example, has revolved around rival analyses about the nature of guerrilla warfare and predictions about the effects of alternative ways of dealing with it. In China policy the debate has centered on the analysis of the nature of Chinese Communism, its capacity to change Chinese society, and whether or not it was a "passing phase," as well as on predictions about the effects of the rival policies of "isolating" Communist China or maintaining an "open door" for a lessening of hostility and eventual accommodation. And so it has been in most policy debates, the crux of the debate in each instance turning on an analysis of the factors bearing on the problem and on predictions about the consequences of alternative ways of dealing with it.

More and better knowledge of the kind that permits accurate prediction is undoubtedly the most important single thing that is needed for the improvement of foreign policy. But here again, there is no quick or easy solution. If there was a wide and obvious gap between the pool of basic knowledge available in the universities, say, and what was actually used in informing governmental decisions, something dramatic might be done. But this particular gap, the gap between the knowledge of the experts in government and experts outside, is infinitesimal. Take, for example, the field of "Sovietology." The great body of what is known about the Soviet Union and the workings of Soviet society is shared, and subscribed to, by Soviet specialists within and outside the government. By and large, in fact, the personnel themselves are interchangeable and frequently do shift back and forth. What disagreements there are in the field of Sovietology are not between government and academic experts, but between one group of specialists cutting across both government and academia and another, also cutting across both government and academia. What is really remarkable is how small the area of disagreement is, how accurate are their judgments about Soviet reactions and behavior, and how few are their failures at prediction.

THE POLICY PLANNING STAFF

New and better knowledge is needed, but how can it be developed? Certainly the attempts to institutionalize the effort within government have not been very fruitful. It was this need for knowledge and foresight, according to Dean Acheson, that led General Marshall when he was Secretary of State to establish in 1947 the Policy Planning Staff, a group of about a dozen top-level specialists under an assistant secretary.[2] But in practice the Policy Planning Staff did not work out to be the panacea some had hoped for. It proved to be a useful pool of talent that could be tapped in time of crisis—as its second chief, Paul Nitze, for example, was pulled out for the negotiations after Mossadegh and his government nationalized oil in Iran. Its members have also contributed "think piece" memoranda, which have been neither better nor worse, on the average, than similar thoughtful memoranda written in the action bureaus, in the intelligence agencies, or by outside scholars and writers. But none of this, no matter how well done, fulfills the concept of a "planning" staff, and yet beyond this the Policy Planning Staff has done very little.

What is "planning"? Men building a dam or a bridge can plan in a long range and very precise sense. They can predict the forces that the dam or bridge must withstand and deter-

[2] Dean Acheson, "The President and the Secretary of State," in the The Secreary of State, Don K. Price, ed., for the American Assembly, (1960), p. 48.

mine with great accuracy the materials and strength needed for each part of the structure. In building a dam or a bridge, men can also draw blueprints and develop a schedule for the work to be done that will permit them to specify months in advance the exact dates on which cement, for example, should be ordered and delivered. Some military planning is also of this nature, such as providing port facilities and hospitals and stockpiles of ammunition and so on. Beyond the field of logistics, however, military planning is limited, for the fundamental reason that there is an enemy who has some choice in the matter, too. In war, the only long-range "planning" that can be done apart from logistics is the making of very broad strategic choices.

Long-range planning in foreign affairs is more similar to this kind of military planning than it is to either logistics planning or the kind of planning used to build a dam or a bridge. It is, essentially, analyzing the nature of the problem and making broad strategic choices for dealing with it. Secretary Dulles's 1957 speech about Communist China, which argued for a strategy of isolating the Chinese Communists, was one strategic choice for example. In the Kennedy Administration, the "open door" speech of 1963, which argued for an alternative strategy of "firmness and flexibility" leading toward an eventual accommodation, was another strategic choice. The choice in Vietnam policy was how to treat guerrilla warfare, as we have said—as fundamentally a political problem or as fundamentally a military problem.

Short-range planning in foreign affairs is working out the moves and countermoves in the midst of an ongoing situation, of developing instructions for an ambassador or orders for the fleet. Should the United States move troops into Thailand in response to the Communists' violation of the cease-fire in Laos, and if so what will the Communists then do? Should the United States use an air strike to take out the Soviet missiles in Cuba, confine its action to diplomatic moves, or begin with a blockade? In China policy should the United States lift travel restrictions on Americans, push for

Chinese participation in disarmament talks, and recognize Mongolia, and if so, what will be the Chinese response?

Both the making of broad strategic choices in foreign affairs and this shorter-range form of making contingency calculations of move and countermove are at the political heart of policy making. Consequently, the truth of the matter is that both these kinds of "planning" are done at several places at once—by the advocates of the rival policies and their allies. In the Laos crisis of 1962, for example, one set of plans of what the United States should do if the Communist side continued to violate the cease-fire in spite of our having put troops in Thailand was prepared in the Pentagon and another was prepared by the Bureau of Far Eastern Affairs and their allies in the State Department's Intelligence Bureau. In the struggle over Vietnam policy, one strategic concept for fighting the guerrillas was developed out of a group effort—the work of the British advisors in Saigon (who applied the lessons learned in suppressing the guerrilla terrorism in Malaya), the people in the Intelligence Bureau at the State Department and in the White House, and the military people at the Special Forces center at Fort Bragg. But all this planning was overridden by the planning for traditional warfare that took place in the military headquarters at Saigon. In the Congo crisis, planning usually took place in the Bureau of African Affairs, but every now and again it was done elsewhere—in the bureau responsible for UN affairs, in the Intelligence Bureau, and occasionally, to be completely accurate, in the office of Senator Dodd.

At one time or another, the Policy Planning Staff planned in this sense in its role as ally of one or another set of advocates, but it has succeeded in being the *principal* advocate and planner in very few cases. The Multilateral Force for NATO and the earlier Developmental Loan Fund are two outstanding examples, and it is instructive of the politics of statecraft that both these agencies were bureaucratic orphans, matters that cut across the regular responsibilities of both the regional and the functional offices of the State Department.

POSSIBLE IMPROVEMENTS

Policy is made in a political process for good and sufficient reasons, and so long as these basic reasons persist, attempts at institutionalizing planning or foresight or wisdom are likely to fail. Some improvements, of course, can be made. A climate of receptivity to new ideas and knowledge can be created rather easily, for example, and creating such a climate of receptivity can have important consequences as people are encouraged to experiment with new ideas and to put them forward. Although it was partly nullified in the State Department by the attitude at the top, President Kennedy established this climate of receptivity at the beginning of his Administration very quickly. His actions showed that he was reading people's memos, and he called "little" men on the phone, all of which created an excitement that the bureaucracy had not known for many years. Government can also do more to encourage research and the development of new knowledge in political and social affairs. The Defense Department, for example, spends billions of dollars supporting research in the physical sciences, but it was not until the Kennedy Administration that the State Department obtained money for supporting research in foreign affairs. Even then Congress appropriated less than $100,000 for the purpose. Something might also be done to direct research and the work of increasing basic knowledge to questions that are more immediately relevant to the issues of foreign policy. Much of the work in the universities on social, political, and economic matters, for example, would benefit from a better understanding of the issues as the policy maker must view them. Not only would the results be of more utility to governmental decisions, but the research itself would benefit in a purely scholarly sense by a sharpening of its perspectives.

Important though the results of these kinds of effort might be in the long run, the immediate results would not be any very dramatic improvement in United States foreign policy. The making of foreign policy is a groping effort at understanding the nature of the evolving world around us. It is a painful sorting out of our own goals and purposes. It is a tentative, incremental experimentation with various means for achieving these purposes. It is an unremitting argument and debate among various constituencies about all these questions and an attempt to build a consensus on how the United States as the United States should decide on these questions and what action it should take. None of these several activities is the kind that will yield to organizational or institutional gimmicks.

PERSONNEL

One other possible area for improvement in United States foreign policy is people. Other things being equal, good people make good foreign policy and better people make better foreign policy.

The people who make foreign policy are, as we have seen, widely varied—the press, interest groups, attentive publics, congressmen—but within the Executive branch itself, where something concrete could be done, the "people who make foreign policy" fall into two general groups. One group is made up of career officials in the foreign service, the civil service, and the military services. The other group is composed of Presidential appointees and the people they bring with them—the group of officials who make up an administration.

There was a time when the quality and training of people in the career group were undoubtedly not as good as they should have been. But much has been done in the years since World War II, not only to broaden the foreign service and the career civil service, but to improve the knowledge and training of everyone concerned with foreign affairs and national security, civilian and military. Pay, retirement, and other benefits have made a government career more attractive. Qualifications have been raised. Mid-career training is provided, not only at the Foreign Service Institute and the service war colleges, but also by new legislation that permits agencies to send officials to private universities for special training. The task of maintaining high standards in the career services and of seeking new ways to improve training is never completely ended, but by and large the United States can be proud of its career services, both civilian and military. The people in them are able, well trained, and dedicated professionals, and although there are things that can be done to help them and to maintain the present high standards, none will bring any marked improvement in the quality of foreign policy.

The "front men"

The second group, the people who make up an administration, are the "front men" whose functions were discussed in Chapter 2. It is their function, to repeat, to be the *advocates* of policy—to represent the President to the career specialists and the career specialists to the President; to build a consensus for policy within the Executive branch, on Capitol Hill, and with the press and public; and to do battle for the substance of policy. By the nature of his job, the front man takes the political heat and is, in consequence, expendable.

The front man as "in-and-outer"

It is the high expendability of the front men—as well as the fact of their identification with a particular President and his administration, who are, after all, impermanent—that accounts for their being dubbed the "in-and-outers."[3] Unlike J. Edgar

[3] Credit for the term seems to belong jointly to Richard E. Neustadt and Adam Yarmolinsky—both of them "in-and-outers" themselves. See Neustadt's "White House and Whitehall," already cited on p. 2, and Adam Yarmolinsky, "Ideas into Programs," both of which appear in *The Public Interest* 2 (Winter 1966).

Hoover who headed the FBI for over forty years, there is no example of someone who was always "in" in the foreign affairs field in the sense of holding high office. But the term "in-and-outers" does have some misleading connotations, especially the implication that there is a ladder and that men come in and out to gradually increasing responsibilities and experience. Many do. Dean Acheson started as Assistant Secretary of the Treasury under Roosevelt. He went out in a disagreement over fiscal policy, then came back as Assistant Secretary for Economic Affairs in the State Department. Later he was Assistant Secretary for Congressional Relations, then Under Secretary, and out again. Finally, he came back as Secretary of State under President Truman. W. Averell Harriman started very near the top, but he gained in experience by serving in every Democratic Administration since Roosevelt's, being out of the foreign affairs area of government only during the Eisenhower years. Dean Rusk was Assistant Secretary for UN Affairs in the Truman Administration, and Deputy Under Secretary and Assistant Secretary for Far Eastern Affairs. He went out to head the Rockefeller Foundation and then came back again to be Secretary of State. Other, completely random, examples of in-and-outers are Henry L. Stimson, Chester Bowles, Allen Dulles, Paul Nitze, Adolf Berle, George W. Ball, McGeorge Bundy, Arthur H. Dean, Robert A. Lovett, Douglas Dillon, J. Kenneth Galbraith, John J. McCloy, and John McCone.

Some front men come in only once. Henry A. Wallace, for example, held three positions the first time in—Secretary of Agriculture, Vice President, and Secretary of Commerce—but he never came back once he went out. Eisenhower's Secretary of Agriculture, Ezra Taft Benson, and his Secretary of Defense, Charles E. Wilson, had never held government posts before their appointments as cabinet members; neither had Kennedy's Secretary of Defense, Robert S. McNamara.

Where do the front men come from? Many have come from Wall Street—Henry L. Stimson, James V. Forrestal, Paul Nitze,

Douglas Dillon. Some come from politics—G. Mennen Williams and James F. Byrnes. Some come from the law—Dean Acheson, George W. Ball, and Arthur H. Dean. Some come from a combination of law and politics—Adlai E. Stevenson. Some have come from business and industry—Charles E. Wilson, Averell Harriman, and Chester Bowles, the last two having an interim period in politics. Some have come from academia and the foundation world—Dean Rusk, McGeorge Bundy, Adolf Berle, Philip C. Jessup, and J. Kenneth Galbraith. Some have come from the career service—Robert Murphy, who went pretty steadily up and went out only on retirement. Coming from the career service, Murphy was an "up-and-outer" rather than an "in-and-outer." George F. Kennan was both. He rose to prominence as Ambassador to the Soviet Union and head of the Policy Planning Staff, left for an academic post, and returned as Ambassador to Yugoslavia. Some of the front men are really "up-and-backers" or "up-and-to-one-siders"—Charles E. Bohlen, for example, who was at the heart of policy making in the Truman years, sat out the Eisenhower Administration as Ambassador to Manila, and returned to the heart of policy making in the Kennedy Administration. There are also the "in-and-outers" and "up-and-backers" from the military—Maxwell Taylor, James Gavin, Walter Bedell Smith, George C. Marshall, Lucius Clay—all of whom held high civilian office after reaching prominent military positions.

These front men as we have said are key in making foreign policy effective. They are the ones who kick and push and shove to get the government to recognize a problem and face up to the policy choices rather than drift in indecision. They are the ones who sponsor policy alternatives, who do the work of enlisting support, arguing, selling, persuading, and building a consensus around a particular course of action. It is their leadership or lack of it that determines whether a decision will be vigorously or indifferently carried out.

The effectiveness of foreign policy depends peculiarly on the front men. If their quality, training, and progressive experience can be improved, so will foreign policy. The nation should clearly pay careful attention to their upbringing, care, and feeding.

But here again there is no simple solution. To an American, for example, the British parliamentary system seems to provide a neat solution to the problem of providing an obvious ladder, early selection, and progressive experience for policy leaders. There is an opportunity to start early. Men may run for parliament from any district without residence requirements, and an able man may get a seat while still very young. There is opportunity to work up. The member sits on the back benches and learns, eventually earning a position as parliamentary undersecretary where he can work from inside the great departments. If he is an apt pupil with sufficient luck, sooner or later he will get a Cabinet post. And there is provision for the "out" period that permits him to develop and work in the field of his major interest. When his party is out of power he still has a seat in parliament from which he can participate, study, and follow developments in his special field. Most importantly of all, there is the clear expectation on his part, by his constituency, his colleagues, and his adversaries, that he will in fact be back.

To an American all this seems a marvelous system for the upbringing of front men. But to an Englishman, on the other hand, it does not always look quite so wonderful. To him the system sometimes seems to ensure that there will never be any new blood. Responsibility for policy making alternates between two small groups of familiar people in a tight procedure that works against any possibility of new faces and fresh ideas. More than one Englishman has commented on how difficult it would be for a new British government to bring into high and influential posts such a glittering array of new, young, and vigorous people full of verve and fresh ideas that the Kennedy Administration assembled. The old, familiar "shadow Cabinet," they complain, merely replaces the old, familiar Cabinet—and back and forth in a dull minuet. Once in a while a single new face can be brought in, but only by the ponderous device of forcing a resignation in a safe seat and holding a by-election or by having the man elevated to the peerage and given a seat in the House of Lords.

In the United States there are a few things that might be done to improve matters. The attractions of going "in" or "up" can be increased, and the risks of having no place to go "out" or "back" can be reduced. Perhaps other measures can be taken to ease the lot and improve the incentive of the "front men." But it is difficult to conceive of any very radical changes in their recruitment, training, or conditions of servitude. So here again the somewhat pessimistic conclusion seems inescapable—there is no easy route to dramatic improvement.

CONCLUSION

And so it goes. Knowledge can and should be increased and made available at all levels of participation, inside and outside the government and among the attentive publics—but the improvement in foreign policy will be slow. Communications and the flow of information among all participants at all levels can and should be improved, and the results will be good but not dramatic. Policy is made in a political process involving debate among rival advocates before a variety of constituencies, and the wisest course is probably to concentrate on trying to maximize the strengths of the system rather than change it. Secrecy should in general be mistrusted, although it is sometimes necessary. Expertise should be given a full hearing, but experts themselves should be watched, at least for the narrowness of their interest. Deliberate heed should be paid to the role of the process itself, the need for debate, and the involvement of all those who have a legitimate interest or contribution. The best way to improve policy, in a word, is probably to conduct it with an eye, but a highly discriminating eye, to the realities of the political process by which it is made.

"Policy faces inward as much as outward," we said at the end of the first chapter of this book, "seeking to reconcile conflicting goals, to adjust aspirations to available means, and to accommodate the different advocates of these competing goals and aspirations to one another. It is here that the essence of policy making seems to lie, in a process that is in its deepest sense political." Facing this reality means, first, that most of the turmoil, conflict, pulling, and hauling in the making of foreign policy will continue. Vast increases in knowledge, in the capacity to predict the consequences of foreign policy action, will greatly improve the effectiveness of policy. But it will not change the appearance of turmoil. It will mean only that those matters on which knowledge has been improved will be handled by technicians, down the line, leaving the top policy makers to devote their time to matters on which knowledge is still inadequate or on which the issue is conflicting interests rather than disagreement over means. The policy handled at the top will continue to be made in a political process, with all the familiar turmoil.

Facing this reality, second, means that improvements are most likely to come not in trying to find ways to escape the fact that the process is political, which seems foredoomed to failure, but to accept it and to seek ways to make sure that the process serves its political functions, when it faces inward, as well as its policy functions, when it faces outward. President Kennedy, for example, failed to ensure that all viewpoints were fully represented in the deliberations on the Bay of Pigs; in so doing he denied himself expert knowledge that might have prevented the disaster. President Johnson could not avoid knowing the views of those opposed to the Vietnam War, but he sought to maneuver around the opposition, rather than reconcile the differing views, and in so doing he divided the country as it has not been divided since the Civil War.

Here, too, there are no gimmicks that will transform the system, and seeking improvements that face the reality that the process is political will probably bring no dramatic results.

At one stage in the Vietnam struggle, for example, a group of opponents of President Johnson's Vietnam policy—congressional leaders, eminent professors, and former high officials —met in New York to consider constitutional and other changes that would give Congress more power over foreign policy and put restraints on the Presidency to prevent future Vietnams. All recognized that the ultimate restraint planned by the founding fathers of the American republic, the power of the purse, had failed. The power of the purse works well in most matters, but not in war. Few senators and congressmen will vote against military appropriations in a war, even in a war like the one in Vietnam which they oppose. The political argument against them is too powerful, "You may oppose the war, but we are in it, and a vote against military appropriations now means taking the guns out of the hands of young men who are being killed." Many proposals were suggested, and rejected. One Senator suggested a constitutional amendment prohibiting the President from sending more than 5,000 troops abroad without an act of Congress. Another pointed out that a President could get the United States just as inextricably involved with 5,000 men as he could with 50,000. During the alliance negotiations between France and Great Britain prior to World War I, someone recalled, the French ambassador was asked how many British troops should be stationed in France prior to hostilities. "Just one," he is supposed to have replied, "and if war comes, we will take care to see that he is killed."

Proposals to force the President to consult Congress in advance were also considered. But present in everyone's mind were those crises, such as the Cuban missile crisis, which can be met only with speed and secrecy, and it was the congressmen present, above all, who felt most strongly that such a crisis could not be handled effectively by a congressional committee.

The only possibility, in fact, is to strengthen congressional powers not to veto an upcoming policy, but to conduct a thorough postmortem on past policy. The hearings conducted on Vietnam, on President Johnson's intervention in the Dominican Republic, and on the Tonkin Gulf resolution are examples. These were conducted after the events and could not have prevented them. But if every President knew that Congress would conduct a searching, thorough, objective postmortem on every single one of his major foreign policy decisions, he would have the strongest of incentives to see that every shade of expert opinion was consulted, that the views and interests of every major constituency were fully considered, and that the consequences of proceeding without reconciliation of the opposing views were calculated and weighed. The result might be an improvement, but it would not be particularly dramatic.

"DEMOCRACY" IN THE MAKING OF FOREIGN POLICY

One final word should be added. All these considerations have been about the effectiveness of foreign policy, not whether it was "good" or "bad." Whether foreign policy is effective turns on whether or not the government recognizes an emerging problem and faces up to it, whether or not the policy adopted is in fact the alternative most likely to achieve the desired goal, and whether or not the decision is vigorously and efficiently carried out. The results, however, can be either "good" or "bad" depending on one's particular goals and interests—which is why the making of foreign policy is a political matter. This involvement of the values and interests of the different segments of society in turn raises the question of "democracy" in the making of foreign policy.

The relative openness of the process of policy making, the variety of constituencies, and the strain toward consensus provide at least for the possibility that different views of what is "good" and what is "bad" will be heard. By and large the very existence of these different constituencies—including the constituency of the press with its peculiar interest in conflict and disagreement—ensures that most of the major foreign policies will continue to be decided in the relatively open process of conflict and consensus building and that the full range of different views will be represented even when the number of participants is restricted for reasons of security. But this still permits an occasional decision to be made in an inner circle that excludes major constituencies and major bodies of knowledge and expertise—as the Bay of Pigs so vividly illustrates. President Kennedy used to say that a domestic failure would hurt the country but that a failure in foreign affairs could kill it. Yet it is in foreign affairs that "closed" decisions like the Bay of Pigs are most possible, for the President's power to take independent action is far greater in the field of foreign affairs than it is in domestic matters.

Once burned by the Bay of Pigs, President Kennedy made sure that his decisions in the Cuban missile crisis, in sending troops to Thailand in the Laos crisis, and so on were taken only with the full range of both the interested constituencies and the relevant expertise, even though secrecy demanded that the decision be "closed" in a public sense. But an egocentric President, a man who saw himself as infallible and whose thirst for power had excluded independent-minded men from his administration or muted their voices, could make a particular decision without considering the range of constituencies at any time and could succeed in making the process itself much less open than it normally is, at least for a time. One wonders, in fact, whether this is the story of Vietnam.

Once more there is no simple or easy solution. No constiutional amendment will give this guarantee, and neither will reorganizing and strengthening the National Security Council. Any other alternative—such as giving Congress a more direct role—would probably make it impossible to move quickly and effectively in time of crisis. The Cuban missile crisis, to repeat, could not have been effectively handled by a congressional committee.

As a practical matter, the nearest thing we have to a guarantee that foreign policy will continue to be made in a relatively open, "democratic" process of conflict and consensus building is the way that men ordinarily get to be President of the United States. A man who can last through the long, hard climb up the ladder of American politics to the pinnacle of the Presidency must have an urge to power. But it is also unlikely that a man who comes within reach of the Presidency in the normal way would lack at the center of his character a sympathy for the range of values among Americans and a natural instinct for the political process of consensus building. For the buffeting and merciless public scrutiny of political life in America does expose the weakness of human character, and the electorate responds accordingly.

Even so, the prize of the Presidency has attracted men of all types—men of brilliance, men of monumental mediocrity, and men of almost neurotic vanity and egocentricity. The accidents of history being what they are, men of all three types have actually achieved the prize and become President. This being so, how can limits be set on the President and all the other holders of power—military, civilian, industrial, and financial—as a practical matter while still preserving the nation's capacity to act decisively? How can the interests of all the people be ensured and all the knowledge and expertise that is availabe be guaranteed its rightful role in the making of policy?

This is an age in which the youth have called for "participatory democracy," and in a sense this is the one sure answer. The only way of ensuring that the interests of all the people, as well as the full range of knowledge and expertise, are considered in the making of policy, is for all to recognize the essential point that policy making is a political process and for every individual person who cares about the answer to these questions himself to participate in the process.

As Alexis de Tocqueville observed so long ago, it is more difficult for a whole people to rise above itself than a single person, and a democracy may therefore be more bigoted and prejudiced and sometimes even more unjust than a wise and enlightened king or dictator. But providing for a wise and enlightened king or dictator is chancy at best, and with all its faults and drawbacks, a true democracy is at least open —open in the sense that there are avenues for participation, ways in which active individuals can work to change a particular policy or the structure of the entire society. Achieving change is frustratingly slow, consuming of time and energy. But when it is achieved through this political process of conflict and consensus building, it has one virtue—that the outmoded and discredited status quo cannot return. For the fact that the political process of change is really a change in fundamental social attitudes means that change so wrought acquires the permanency of the status quo it replaced.

INDEX

Eisenhower, Dwight D. *(Continued)*
  "military-industrial complex" and,
    3, 139
  military policy of, 7, 31, 51, 119
  NSC and, 155–156, 173
  organization of government and.
    1, 156, 160
  Vietnam and, 29, 80
Elections, 91–98
Engels, George, 53–54
Europe, American troops in, 81
  U.S. policy toward, 129

Federal Bureau of Investigation (FBI),
  9
Foreign aid, 126
Foreign Intelligence Advisory Board,
  65
Foreign Relations Committee, 73, 77,
  81
Foreign Service, 42–48, 180–181
Forrestal, James V., 49, 154, 182
Forrestal, Michael V., 2
Fox, William R., 131 n., 132
France, in Vietnam, 29–30
"Front Men," 181–185
Fulbright, J. William, 23, 76, 77,
  102, 165

Gaither Committee, 7
Galbraith, J. K., 182
Gavin, James, 183
Geneva agreements (1962), 28, 111
  See also Laos
Gilpatrick, Roswell, 163
Goldwater, Barry, 76, 78, 103
Goodell, Charles, 75–76
Great Britain, 30, 184
Great Depression, 13
Grey, Gordon, 156
Gruening, Ernest, 26, 77
Guerilla warfare, 13, 125, 128

Harriman, W. Averell, 165, 182
Harrison, Benjamin, 164
Higgins, Marguerite, 103
Hitler, 13, 107, 132
Ho Chi Minh, 30
Hoover, J. Edgar, 9, 65, 182

Hudson Institute, 10
Hunt, H. L., 149
Huntington, Samuel R., 118

Indonesia, 59, 120, 124, 140
Institute for Defense Analysis, 10
Interest groups, 105–109
"Invisible Government," 60
Iran, 176
Irish in America, 70

Jackson, Henry, 159, 161
Japan, 70
Jessup, Philip C., 183
Johnson, Lewis, 169
Johnson, Lyndon, 145
  CIA and, 65
  Vietnam and, 14, 28, 30, 77, 115,
    119, 126, 186; bombing of
    North Vietnam, 21, 22–23, 29,
    102, 103, 170; and Gulf of Ton-
    kin resolution, 24, 26
Joint Chiefs of Staff, 7, 48
Judd, Walter H., 53
Junkers, 53

Katanga, 74–75, 76, 124
Keating, Kenneth, 74–75, 76, 78
Kennan, George F., 141, 157 n., 183
Kennedy, Edward, 149
Kennedy, John F., 2, 19, 145, 189
  Bay of Pigs invasion and, 59, 98,
    130, 186
  Cabinet and, 30, 35
  China and, 82, 177
  CIA and, 65
  Cuba and, 1
  Defense Department and, 6
  election of, 90, 91, 94, 97
  Laos and, 27, 28, 30, 80, 103,
    111–112, 119, 126
  NSC and, 1
  policy making and, 1, 15, 20, 143,
    179
  on Presidency, 17
  press and, 114
  State Department and, 46, 160–
    171
  Vietnam and, 1, 13
Kennedy, Robert, 75, 77, 102

Vandenberg, Arthur H., 80
Versailles, Treaty of, 22
Viet Minh, 29
Vietnam, 17, 79, 107, 126, 189
  bombing of the North, 21, 22–23,
    88–89, 102, 103, 133, 170
  Buddhist crisis of 1963, 77, 103
  Eisenhower and, 80
  Johnson policy on, 14, 24, 26, 28–
    29, 71, 80, 119, 186, 188
  Kennedy policy on, 1–2, 6, 13, 77,
    98
  military policy and, 41, 54, 128,
    177, 178
  Nixon policy on, 75–76, 104
  policy making and, 30, 37, 121,
    137, 175
  press and, 110, 115

Wagner Labor Relations Act, 93

Wallace, Henry A., 182
War Department, 42
Washington, D.C., 2–3
Washington Post, 8, 123
Weber, Max, 173
West Point (Military Academy), 52,
  56
Westmoreland, William, 39
Williams, G. Mennen, 33, 35, 183
Wilson, Charles E., 182
Wilson, Woodrow, 22, 85, 118, 126
Wisconsin, Congressmen from, 72
Wolfers, Arnold, 132
Women Strike for Peace, 9
World War I, 187
World War II, 13, 56, 58, 133
Wriston Report, 42, 45

Yarmolinsky, Adam, 181 n.